Embroider Your Clothes and Linens

Take your clothes and linens (whether store-bought or homemade) and transform them into objects of beauty with Gina Célestin's marvelous embroidery designs.

Here is a wide variety of needlework projects — using many styles, patterns, and techniques, both traditional and modern — that will teach you how to embroider a garden on the sheer sleeves of a peasant blouse; turn a classic linen tablecloth into a unique heirloom; put monograms on your towels, intricate borders on your skirts, leaves and swirls on your placemats and napkins, and wild roses on an evening gown. You'll do fashionable white-on-white embroidery, Portuguese embroidery, and Spanish blackwork. You'll use cross-stitch to make a tea cloth, hemstitching to decorate a shirtdress, and beading to embellish a cocktail dress.

You'll find everything you need to know to complete the projects: a stitching key, working design and photograph, and complete step-by-step instructions for each project; information on needles, threads, and fabrics; complete how-to's for doing

(Continued on back flap)

Embroider Your Clothes and Linens

Gina Célestin

BOBBS-MERRILL

INDIANAPOLIS/NEW YORK

THIS BOOK *is dedicated with love and affection
to my late mother, who inspired me in my
artistic endeavor.*

G.C.

Library of Congress Cataloging in Publication Data

Célestin, Gina.
    Embroider your clothes and linens.

    1. Embroidery.   I.   Title.
TT770.C44   746.4′4   77-15445
ISBN 0-672-52073-7

Designed by Bernard Schleifer
Manufactured in the United States of America

FIRST PRINTING

The velvet pants shown on
page 116 were designed by
Jacques Jaunet, Inc.

The designs were drawn by the author.
All other drawings were done by Betsy Milam.

Contents

2015969

Introduction

THE EMBROIDERY REVIVAL is sweeping the country. Now anyone can easily add personal and creative touches to everything they wear, from everyday workshirts to luxurious evening dresses. During the great do-it-yourself revolution, the return of the art of embroidery is only natural. Embroidery gives our wearing apparel the personal touch and can make simple garments look expensive and individual.

Good taste and beauty in the garments we wear cannot be achieved with money alone. Many of the touches that add beauty and elegance to our clothes and linens are quite inexpensive. The creative use of embroidery costs very little—there is only the cost of floss or yarn, which is relatively inexpensive. The main ingredient is style. You must find and develop your own personal style. This book was developed to stimulate, inspire and help you create and achieve the results you want.

The art of embroidery has adjusted through the ages for modern needs. Today's woman no longer does the ancient gossamer needlework requiring long hours of work. The amount of time spent on a project is important; we no longer want to devote a great deal of time to one single activity. Speed calls for more rapid techniques. Most of the designs in this book will not involve a huge investment of time.

This book treats the art of embroidery as it applies to decorating clothes and linens. As you will see, this is within everybody's reach. You will learn how to handle the most effective combinations of fabric, thread, design, color and stitches in order to produce the most beautiful and perfect work. You will learn how easy and what fun it is to create your own designs to decorate your dresses, sweaters, blouses, shirts and linens.

The purpose of this book is to inspire you to create beautiful embroidered clothes and linens on your own—easily, enjoyably and at great savings! Here you will be shown all the methods and techniques you need to know (enlarging your designs, transferring your designs onto fabric, choosing materials, mastering stitches, learning monograms). This is the kind of knowledge you will need to stimulate your imagination to create beautiful work.

Most importantly, you will learn many easy ways to change your clothes and linens quickly and imaginatively so that old things look like new and new ones are truly unique.

Part I

Before You Start

1. Fabrics, working materials and tools

It is impossible to do really fine embroidery without the proper materials and equipment. Basically, the three major necessities are fabric, needle and thread. There are, however, additional tools that help ensure neat and professional-looking results.

FABRICS

So long as the proper techniques are followed for the particular material, there is hardly a fabric that doesn't lend itself to beautiful hand embroidery. You can use anything from delicate sheers to cottons, silks, synthetics, velvets, denim and wool.

Linen, with its long-wearing fiber, has been the traditional background fabric for centuries. In case you are wondering why, just witness the magnificent crewel-embroidered overshirts, coats, coverlets and hangings displayed in museums. They remain in almost perfect condition. Linen, now generally treated to be crease-resistant, is still a prime material, whether for use as a classic dress or tablecloth. Linen is ideal for embroidery work because of its beauty, durability and the ease with which it can be stitched.

Although linen is an excellent material for embroidery, there are many other suitable materials just waiting for the touch of embroidery to make them special. In general, fabrics with a certain amount of body that are firmly but not too tightly woven are the best choices. This leaves a wide variety of materials from which to choose. Here in this book you'll find, for example, a white silk shirt, velvet pants and a T-dress, in addition to several linen tablecloths, table runners and other linens.

You'll learn professional tricks for embroidering successfully with all these fabrics. With pile fabrics, for example, you'll learn how to work the design from a tissue that has been basted to it. You'll see how stabilizing the area with a batiste underlining keeps knit fabrics from stretching, and you'll be able to do charming cross-stitch designs with perfect results by stitching over needlepoint canvas and pulling out the threads later.

All of the designs in this book work beautifully on clothes and linens that are already made. Except for the velvet pants and the denim-look T-dress, I worked from scratch. If you care to work from scratch as well, helpful notes will tell you when to start the embroidery and when to seam and hem.

Just one piece of advice: When you take the time and care to beautify your clothes with embroidery, you will, of course, want them to last. So all these designs are meant for classic styles. A simple A-line or shirt-dress, an evening dress with the simplest lines, a wraparound or flared skirt, a traditional silk shirt—all of these are bound to stay in style for years. Avoid extreme styles that go out of fashion in a season or two. The other rule is to keep the background simple. Embroidery would be lost on most prints, and a garment with an intricate cut is ornamentation enough. If you are starting from scratch with any of these designs, remember to keep the pattern and fabric simple. Good materials and classic, unfussy styles will show off your embroidery best.

THREADS

The embroidery designs in this book were done with the following threads, all of which can be found in local needlework and notions stores. Different threads will result in different effects, and you should experiment with any thread that interests you. Threads come in a wide range of colors and the standard brands are reliably colorfast. The main criteria for choosing a thread are that it will slip easily through the fabric and that it will produce the effect you want.

Cotton Embroidery Floss

This is a glossy thread composed of six strands that are easily separated. You may work with all six or with one, two or three strands, depending upon the nature of the design and the kind of effect you wish to achieve. Cotton embroidery floss is sold in skeins.

Mat-Finish Cotton Embroidery Twist

This is a fine, dull-finished cotton that is also sold in skeins.

Pearl Cotton

Pearl cotton, which is a twisted glossy thread, comes in sizes #1, #3, #5 and #8. The higher the number, the finer the thread. The heavier sizes are sold by the skein and the finer sizes come in balls and skeins.

Silk Buttonhole Twist

This twisted thread is known for its beautiful sheen. It is sold in small spools.

Nylon Twist

This thread is a glossy twisted thread that cannot be separated. It is sold in skeins.

Metallic Thread

Shining silver and gold threads produce very special effects. Fabrics to be embroidered with metallic thread should be chosen with care; some metallic threads can be hard on fabrics. The threads are sold in spools.

Invisible Nylon Thread

This is used for beaded embroidery and is sold in spools.

Bulky Embroidery Wool

This wool is heavy wool yarn that cannot be separated. It should, therefore, be used for bold effects. Bulky embroidery wool is sold by the skein.

NEEDLES

The best needles for embroidering on dress fabrics are *crewel needles*. They have sharp points that penetrate easily without leaving a hole, and their long eyes take most threads easily. Crewel needles come in sizes ranging from #1 to #10. The higher the number, the finer the needle and the smaller the eye. They can accommodate everything from fine metallic thread to embroidery floss to heavy embroidery wool. When you buy your embroidery thread, choose the needle that will accommodate your thread without bunching. If the eye is too small, it will wear the thread thin as you work and may even break it. If you are inexperienced at this, you might ask a salesperson at a needlework shop for advice.

The needle chosen should make a clear opening in the fabric. If the thread breaks, the needle is probably too small.

Tapestry needles, which have larger eyes but blunt points, are useful for stitches that are woven on the surface of your work, such as the woven spider web. Their blunt points help prevent splitting and damaging of the threads in the stitches as you weave in and out.

Needles that are long and thin enough to fit through the tiny hole of a bead are used for beading. They are called *beading needles.*

HOOPS

Embroidery always looks neater and more professional when it has been done in a hoop. The hoop keeps the fabric taut so you can place the stitches accurately. Hoops come in many sizes and are made of metal or wood. Wooden hoops are generally better, and a good standard size to work with is 6 inches in diameter. The fabric is placed over the inside hoop and then the outside hoop is placed over both (Figure 1). The fabric is stretched taut and the small screw on the outer hoop is used for adjusting the tension (Figure 2). The only problem with using a hoop is that it sometimes leaves a mark on the fabric (for example, when using pure silk). Linens, heavy cottons and wools are durable and tough; you can press any hoop marks right out of them. For delicate fabrics, though, it's best to pad the hoop with layers of tissue paper or twill tape or even terry cloth before tightening the hoop. Hoops are not to be used on velveteen, velvet, or any pile fabrics because they will flatten the pile. And, of course, hoops can't be used on very small areas, such as collar points, unless you sew the collar onto a larger piece of fabric and place that fabric in the hoop. In general, use the hoop wherever you can. You can even use a hoop on the legs of pants if the inner hoop is small enough to fit inside the width of the leg.

When using a hoop, work the needle straight up and out, keeping one hand above

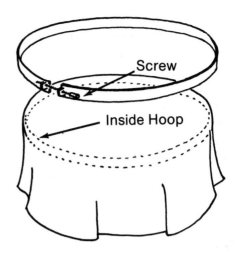

Fig. 1. *Placing fabric in hoop.*

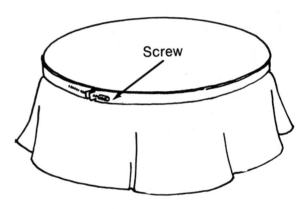

Fig. 2. *Tightening the screw.*

for the down motion and one hand below for the up motion. You should not sew in and out on the surface or you'll stitch the piece out of shape.

OTHER TOOLS

Of great importance to the embroiderer is a good pair of *scissors* with short, sharp blades. These are needed so that you can cut threads accurately and close to the surface. Some embroiderers will want to work with a *thimble.* Although this has been a traditional practice, thimbles are not so commonly used today. If you do use one, it is most important that the thimble fit correctly. Another tool that some embroiderers find useful is a *magnifying glass.* This is perhaps more important for intricate work where stitches are very small. For the most part, the designs in this book don't incorporate tiny stitches. Other requirements are the tools needed for enlarging and transferring the designs, such as *soft* and *hard pencils,* a *fine-tipped marking pen, dressmaker's carbon paper, graph paper, thumbtacks, masking tape,* and a *knitting needle,* depending upon the methods you choose. Read more about enlarging and transferring in chapter 2.

2. Transferring the design to fabric

In PRINCIPLE, the process of transferring the design onto fabric consists of a few simple stages—tracing the design from the book, enlarging it if needed, and then transferring the design to your fabric.

TRACING THE DESIGN

Since you probably don't want to cut the design page out of your book, you will need to transfer the design onto a separate sheet of paper to be used as your pattern. For the designs that have no grid (the ones that are actual size), simply place a piece of tracing paper over the book design, securing the edges with a bit of masking tape so the paper won't shift. Then trace the outlines of the design, being careful to include all details. A felt-tipped marking pen is excellent for this as it won't tear the paper. This can serve as your pattern, unless you would like to transfer the design onto heavier paper. This is actually a good idea; tracing paper has a tendency to tear during the transferring-to-fabric process. Most of the designs in this book, however, have been reduced to fit on the book page, so they will now have to be enlarged to actual size. For these, there is no need to trace the design from the book, since you will have to enlarge the design anyway.

ENLARGING THE DESIGN

All designs with a grid have been marked with the correct scale—each square equals 1 inch (2.5 cm). To enlarge your design first rule a grid with 1-inch (2.5-cm) squares on paper, making the same number of squares as on the original grid in the book. You can use graph paper, which is usually marked in 1-inch (2.5-cm) squares, or rule your own grid on a large sheet of paper. Now you are ready to copy the design onto the large grid, square by square, until it is complete (see Figure 3).

Fig. 3. *Enlarging a design.*

TRANSFERRING THE DESIGN

There are several easy ways to do this. The method you choose should depend on what seems easiest to you and should take into account the fabric onto which you are transferring the design. Sheers, heavy or pile fabrics and knitted fabrics require special techniques. Also, for finer results in cross-stitch designs, a special technique can be followed.

Dressmaker's Carbon Method

This is the easiest and oldest method. The first step is to make sure you are using dressmaker's carbon. Regular carbon paper will smudge. Use dark carbon for light materials, and white or light for dark materials. Next, place your fabric on a flat surface—a table or an ironing board—smooth it out and hold it in place with masking tape, straight pins or thumbtacks. If an ironing board is your surface, cover it with stiff cardboard or wood to provide a hard surface.

Lay the pattern on top of the fabric, positioning it as directed in the instructions. Most projects are accompanied by a diagram which indicates proper placement of the pattern. Hold the pattern in place with masking tape. It is important that the fabric be stretched taut. Slip the dressmaker's carbon under the pattern, face down, and trace around the pattern, using firm pressure. Go over faint lines as needed. To trace around the lines you can use a hard pencil or the tip of a knitting needle.

Method for Sheer Fabrics

This method can be done with organdy, batiste, or any very thin fabric that you can see through. Simply tape or pin the pattern onto a flat surface (a table or ironing board) and lay your fabric over it, right side down. Smooth it out and hold it in place with masking tape or straight pins. Using a soft pencil, trace the design directly onto the fabric. Turn the fabric right side up and you are ready to embroider.

Method for Heavy or Pile Fabrics

For thick wool, velvet, velveteen, terry cloth or any other fabric with a nap or pile, there are two methods from which to choose. For both methods the pattern will be destroyed in the process, so make sure not to use your one and only design. It's best to trace your design and then trace it again onto a working tissue, leaving the original intact to use again.

To do the first method the design should be traced on a soft tissue or fine tracing paper. Lay the design on the right side of the fabric, smooth it out perfectly and baste it into place. Thread a needle with contrasting color thread and sew along the outlines of the design with small running stitches. When the design has been completed, simply tear away the tissue before doing the embroidery. When the embroidery is finished, pull out any basting that shows.

Another similar method is to baste the design tissue to the right side of the fabric and just embroider over it, tearing away the tissue as you embroider or when the embroidery is completed. Here you'll have to pull out little bits of tissue that get caught under or between stitches.

Method for Knit Fabrics

Before transferring a design onto a knit fabric you must stabilize the fabric so it doesn't stretch. For this you must cut a piece of sheer cotton batiste or organdy just a little larger than the embroidery design area. (Make sure the cotton has been preshrunk.) Turn your knit fabric inside out and baste the batiste to the wrong side, exactly where the embroidery is to be. Attach it with small running stitches around the edges and several times across to hold it in place. Turn the knit fabric right side out and transfer the design by any of the methods mentioned.

For Cross-Stitch Designs

To achieve precise, professional results it's a good idea to use a piece of needlepoint canvas as a guide. Simply transfer the design onto your canvas, lay it over the design on your fabric and then baste it in place. Embroider through both layers and pull out the canvas threads when you're done. The results are beautifully even cross-stitches. It's advisable to soak the canvas before using it. This will remove the stiffening and make it easier to pull out the threads later. Dry it flat on a towel and tack down corners to keep square.

REINFORCING THE DESIGN

Regardless of the method used you might want to reinforce the design lines. For a large design that won't be finished at one sitting, for example, you will want to keep the lines from fading off your fabric. You can go over the design with a felt-tipped marking pen in a neutral color, if the fabric is not too delicate, and wherever the embroidery will cover the marking. Always test the marker first to make sure it's colorfast. Another less risky alternative is to sew a small running stitch over the outlines and embroider right over them. You can remove the running stitches later.

3. Stitches

By LEARNING the embroidery stitches in this chapter you will be able to stitch any one of the designs in Part II. The stitches are divided into three categories—outline stitches, background or filling stitches, and spot stitches. While there are no hard and fast rules regarding when to use each stitch, these classifications indicate the best usage.

Examples for all stitches are fully illustrated and explained in the following text. Pick up a piece of linen, some thread and a needle and practice making each stitch as you go along. This is the simplest way to learn new stitches or to just refresh your memory about some old forgotten ones. Notice the letter in parentheses beside each stitch name. This is the code letter for that stitch, and it will appear on the designs accompanying the projects.

OUTLINE STITCHES

Outlining stitches are used to show the limits of the design or shapes. The following are a few of the many outline stitches.

Running Stitch (R)

The basic running stitch is the simplest and easiest of stitches; it is used for both embroi-

dery and hand sewing, for outlines or as a foundation for other stitches (Figure 4). It is done from right to left, with the needle just "running" along the fabric. Simply bring the needle up at point A, down at point B, up at point C, down at point D and so on. Make all stitches equal and the spaces between them equal.

Fig. 4. *Running Stitch.*

Backstitch (U)

The same stitch is used for embroidery and hand sewing, for lines and outlines (Figure 5).

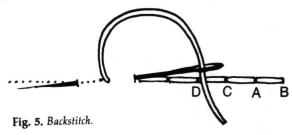

Fig. 5. *Backstitch.*

All stitches should be the same size, for its beauty depends on uniformity. Work stitches from right to left, bringing the needle up a short distance from the beginning of the line at point A, down at point B (the beginning of the line), up at point C, down at point A, up at point D and so on.

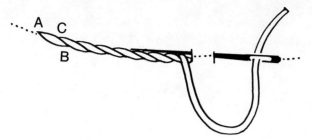

Fig. 7. *Stem Stitch.*

Couching Stitch (K)

This stitch is done for lines and outlines or in close rows for filling (Figure 6). The thread being couched must be held taut to avoid loops and puckers and anchored down at the back of the fabric in some manner. The thread doing the couching is brought up at point A, down at point B, up at point C, down at point D and so on. Stitches must be evenly spaced. Couching is a good way to incorporate decorative threads on fabrics that might not be able to withstand stitching with that thread. For example, some metallic threads stitched on satin would damage the fabric. But metallic thread could be couched on the surface of the satin without damaging it.

Fig. 6. *Couching Stitch.*

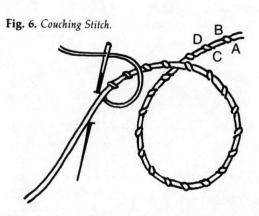

Overcast Stitch (O)

This stitch is used for many types of embroidery, such as for the stems of flowers, outlining and appliqué work (Figure 8). It is also most suitable for working monograms. The stitches are made either very close together to obtain a raised effect, or as shown below. Simply bring the needle up at A, down at point B, up at C, down at D and so on.

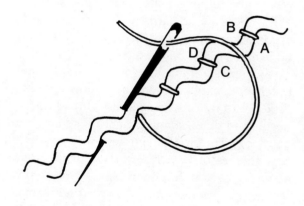

Fig. 8. *Overcast Stitch.*

Stem Stitch (A)

This is a basic decorative stitch used for lines and outlines (Figure 7). The stitch can be worked from right to left, from left to right, or upward and downward. Bring the needle up at point A, then down at point B, up through point C and continue. While stitching, keep your thread below the needle throughout, as shown in the diagram. Be sure to keep all stitches slanting in the same direction. Stem stitches are also used as filling when worked in close rows.

Chain Stitch (C)

This stitch is used for outlining designs that call for a broad edge or as a solid filling when worked in close rows (Figure 9). All rows are started at the top and continued down, forming loops of thread of the same size. Bring the needle up at point A, around, and then down at point B, forming a loop and holding down the loop with your thumb. Bring the needle up at C, making sure that the needle is inside the loop. The chain stitch can also be used as a padding to obtain a raised effect in scallops and monograms. There are a number of variations to the chain stitch, but this is the basic stitch.

Fig. 9. *Chain Stitch.*

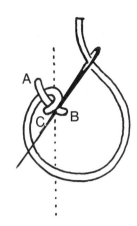

Fig. 10 b.

Fig. 10 c.

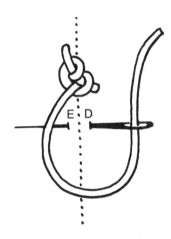

Palestrina Stitch (P)

This stitch is used primarily for lines and outlines (Figures 10 a, b and c). Work the stitches vertically from left to right. Bring the needle up at point A, down at point B and up at point C. Bring the needle around and slip it through the stitch formed by A and B. Bring the needle around again and slip it through the stitch as shown. The needle should be over the looped thread. To start a new stitch bring the needle down at D, up at E and continue. A knotty raised effect is obtained.

Fig. 10 a. *Palestrina Stitch.*

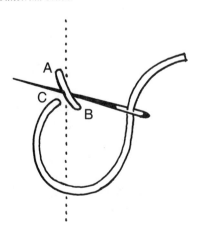

Buttonhole Stitch (B)

This is one of the most versatile stitches and is the basis for other embroidery stitches as well (Figure 11). Also called the *blanket stitch*, it is worked from left to right. Bring the needle up at point A, down at point B and up at

Fig. 11. *Buttonhole Stitch.*

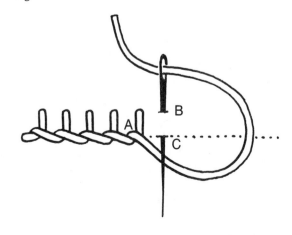

point C directly below B. The buttonhole stitch can be used as edging. A variation of the stitch is the *close buttonhole;* these stitches are made very close together in a solid row for scallops (Figure 12) or around an edge to prevent raveling. In these cases, you stitch up to ½ inch (1.25 cm) from the end and the

extra material is cut away later. Other variations are the *buttonhole wheel* (Figure 13), which radiates from the center, and the *closed buttonhole* (Figure 14).

BACKGROUND OR FILLING STITCHES

Background or filling stitches, as the name indicates, are used to cover an area. Sometimes these stitches create a pattern within a pattern for an interesting textured effect.

Satin Stitch (S)

This is another basic embroidery stitch (Figure 15). Straight stitches are worked close together side by side to cover an area. Bring the needle up at point A, down at point B, up at point C, down at point D and so on. Although this appears to be very easy, the trick is to meticulously follow the design line in order to keep a neat and sharp edge on the shape being filled. Practice is necessary to reach this goal. Changing the direction of the stitches can give a smoother but bolder effect to the work. Stitches can be straight or slanted, but edges must remain even. When making satin stitches, beginners are advised to start at the center of the shape and work toward each end in order to obtain the exact angle. I have a little trick to obtain a bolder effect on large

Fig. 12. *Close Buttonhole in Scallop.*

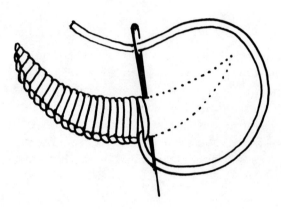

Fig. 13. *Buttonhole Wheel.*

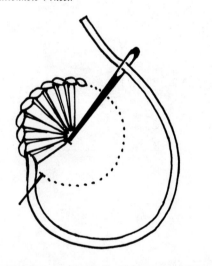

Fig. 14. *Closed Buttonhole Stitch.*

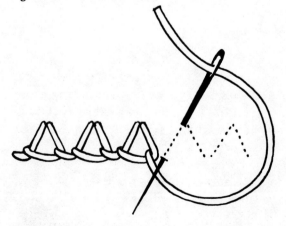

Fig. 15. *Satin Stitch.*

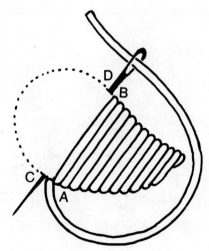

areas. Instead of running the thread under the material, I take my stitch across, pick up a thread or two from the fabric on the opposite side and return, keeping the embroidery thread on the surface, as shown in Figure 16.

Fig. 16. *Satin Stitch.*

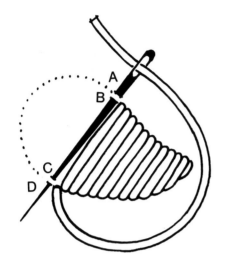

Long and Short Stitches (L)

This name comes from the irregular way of alternating the lengths of the stitches to cover an area. These stitches are worked like regular satin stitches, bringing the needle up at point A, down at B, up at C, down at D and so on, and are mostly used to fill an area too large or irregular to be covered by the regular satin stitch. Sometimes the shapes are not

Fig. 17. *Long and Short Stitches.*

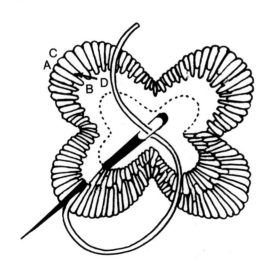

completely covered, as shown in Figure 17. Long and short stitches are particularly useful for shading when worked with different colors or shaded thread. When working in curved shapes, such as petals, it will be impossible to fit each stitch exactly next to the previous one. Every now and again, sneak in an extra stitch in order to obtain a neat finish.

Roman Stitch (Q)

This stitch is often used to fill leaf shapes (Figure 18). Bring the needle up at point A and down at point B, forming a loop. Bring the needle up at point C and down at point D to anchor down the loop. Bring the needle up at point E and continue in this manner until the leaf is covered. Always work from the top to the bottom. Stitches must be worked close together.

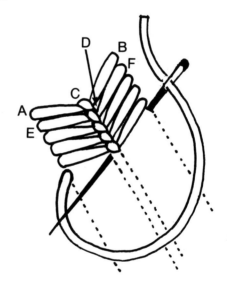

Fig. 18. *Roman Stitch.*

Seeding Stitch (I)

This is simply two backstitches worked in the same holes in any direction and at any angle (Figure 19). It produces an effective filling, whether worked in evenly spaced and sized stitches or irregular stitches at random for a light, airy effect. Bring the needle up at point A, down at point B, up at point A and down at point B.

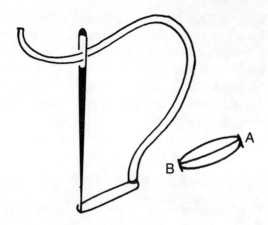

Fig. 19. *Seeding Stitch.*

Darning Stitch (V)

This is another filling stitch and is actually the same as running horizontal lines in and out across the fabric (Figure 20). It consists of long, even running stitches across three or four threads with only one or two threads of material in between each stitch. Bring the

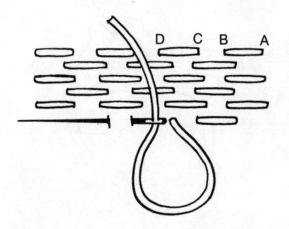

Fig. 20. *Darning Stitch.*

needle up at point A, down at point B, up at point C, down at point D and so on. When you become more experienced with the stitch you will be able to glide the needle through the fabric, collecting several stitches on your needle at once. Rows of darning stitches form a simple "brick pattern."

Arrowhead Stitch (AH)

This stitch is used primarily for filling (Figure 21). Bring needle up at A, down at B and up at C. Point C should be level with point A. Insert needle again in point B. Continue in this manner either vertically or horizontally. AB and BC should form a right angle.

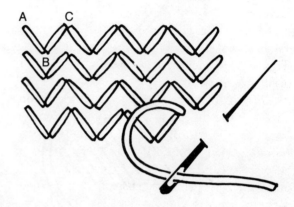

Fig. 21. *Arrowhead Stitch.*

Square Filling Stitch (JS)

This stitch, also called *lattice work*, makes an attractive filling with an open effect. The weaving stitch is just like an ordinary darning stitch used for mending socks but more open (Figure 22). Start with the vertical stitches: Bring the needle up at point A, down at B, up at C, down at D, up at E, down at F and so on until you've covered the area you wish to cover. To do the horizontal stitches, bring the needle up at point a, weave under, over, under, etc., and then bring the needle down at point b. On the next row, weave over, under,

Fig. 22. *Square Filling Stitch.*

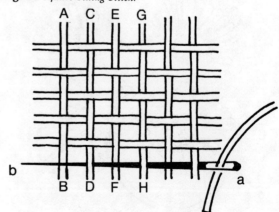

over, etc. Except for the side, most of the stitch is detached from the material as in surface darning. The stitches can be done in straight or diagonal lines.

Cross-Stitch (X)

Though very old, the cross-stitch is always a favorite. It is one of the most popular stitches. It is very simple, consisting of two slanting stitches that cross each other at the center (Figure 23). The cross-stitch can be done in two parts. First, bring the needle up at point A, down at B, up at C, down at D and so on. To complete the cross, and, starting from the opposite direction, bring the needle up at point a, down at point b, up at point c, down at point d and so on. The best results are achieved when you do cross-stitches on needlepoint canvas or even-weave fabric. Also, all stitches should cross in the same way.

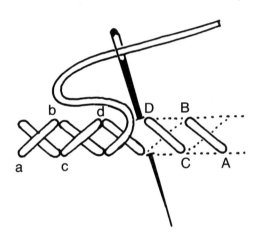

Fig. 23. *Cross-Stitch.*

Fig. 24. *Double Cross-Stitch.*

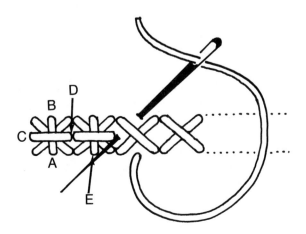

Double Cross-Stitch (XX)

This stitch consists of a cross-stitch with another cross worked over it diagonally (Figure 24). After your cross-stitches are completed, bring the needle up at point A, down at B, up at C, down at D, up at E and so on.

Woven Spider's Web (SW)

The first step in making this stitch is to make the spokes. (Figures 25 a, b and c). Bring the

Fig. 25 a. *Woven Spider's Web.*

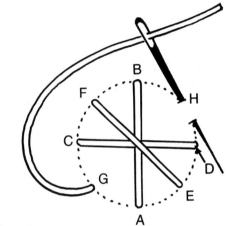

Fig. 25 b.

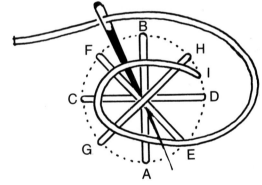

Fig. 25 c.

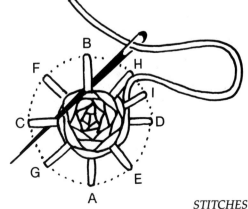

needle up at point A, down at B, and up at C, down at D, up at E, down at F, up at G and down at H. You now have an eight-spoke web. The next step is to do the weaving, but you need an odd number of spokes to do weaving correctly. Bring the needle up at point I (this will be your ninth spoke) and then slide it under the center intersection, forming a loop and keeping the needle inside the loop. Pull to form a knot. Start the weaving at the center, bringing the needle over, under, over, under, etc., each spoke, around and around until the circle is completed.

SPOT STITCHES

These are single stitches that are used for accent or for fillings.

Straight Stitch (T)

This stitch is used singly as an accent or in groups to form shapes, as shown in Figure 26 in which straight stitches are being arranged to form a flower. They are done simply by bringing the needle up at point A, down at B, up at C and so on. Straight stitches can be of any desired length. The main thing is to make firm stitches that are not too long. The stitches can be worked in any direction over the lines to be covered.

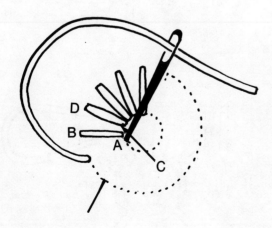

Fig. 26. *Straight Stitch.*

Lazy Daisy Stitch (D)

This is simply a detached chain stitch and is used primarily to make the petals of a flower or leaves (Figures 27 a and b). Simply bring the needle up at A, down at B, forming a loop, and then up at C. Bring the needle down at D to anchor down the loop, and, to make the next stitch, bring the needle up at E, as shown in the figure.

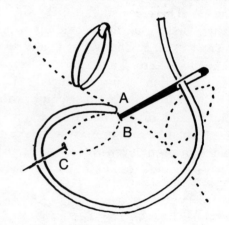

Fig. 27 a. *Lazy Daisy.*

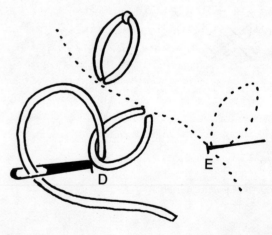

Fig. 27 b.

Long-Tailed Lazy Daisy (DT)

This variation of the lazy daisy is used singly or in groups. Work an ordinary lazy daisy stitch, making the anchoring down stitch (CD in Figure 28) long to look like a tail.

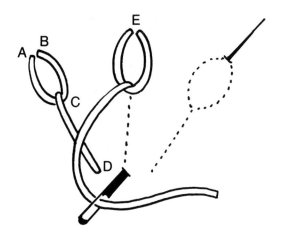

Fig. 28. *Long-Tailed Lazy Daisy.*

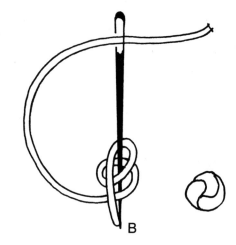

Fig. 29 b.

French Knot (F)

This spot or detached stitch can be scattered like seeding and it may also be used to fill an area, such as the center of a flower. Arrange it in rows in order to fill a space solidly, starting from the edge and working toward the center, or use it anywhere a single dot is required (Figures 29 a and b). Bring the needle up at point A. Wrap the thread around the needle at least once. Insert the needle at B. The number of times you wrap the thread around the needle will determine the size of the knot. It is perhaps best to wrap only once, using thicker thread if a larger knot is desired.

Fig. 29 a. *French Knot.*

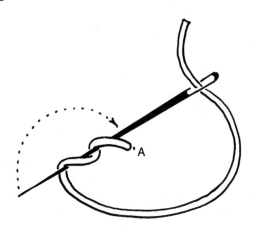

DRAWN THREAD WORK

The drawn thread work techniques are traditionally used to make borders on tablecloths and linens. Basically, drawn thread work consists of decorative stitches worked over loose threads that are left on the fabric after the weft threads have been pulled out.

Hemstitch (J)

This is the most popular of drawn thread stitches. It must, of course, be worked on a fabric that will allow the threads to be easily drawn, such as linen. First determine the width and the length of the area to be drawn. Draw one thread out of the material on either side of the area widthwise. Then draw out the

Fig. 30 a. *Hemstitch.*

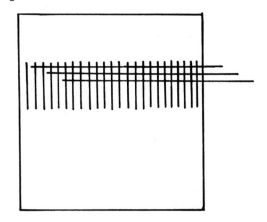

horizontal threads within the area, one by one, until only the vertical threads remain (Figure 30 a). If you are making a hem, the fabric is turned in just up to the edge of the drawn threads and basted. To make the hemstitch, work from left to right and use a blunt tapestry needle and regular sewing thread. Come up at point A, slide the needle

Fig. 30 b.

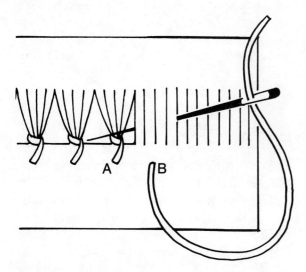

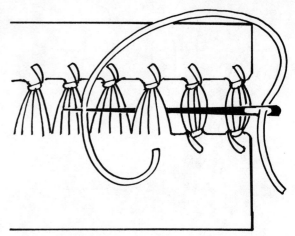

Fig. 31. *Ladder Hemstitch.*

Fig. 32. *Knotted Hemstitch.*

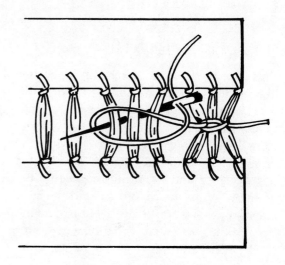

in back of a group of threads (three or more depending on the thickness of your material), wrap the thread around the group and insert the needle into the fabric at point B, which is just to the right of the group of threads just wrapped, as shown in Figure 30 b. Pull the sewing thread tightly and continue working the next group of threads in the same manner.

Ladder Hemstitch (LH)

This stitch is simply a matter of making hemstitches on both sides of the drawn border, as shown in Figure 31.

Knotted Hemstitch (KH)

If you wish, hemstitching can be knotted. After you have completed the ladder work (see Figure 31), slide a tapestry needle under three groups of threads from right to left. Bring the embroidery thread around the needle to form a loop, as shown in Figure 32, and

pull the needle through gently upward to form a knot. The three groups must be pulled tight and the threads between the knots must be taut and even.

Fringing (JF)

This is a very fine way to finish the edges of a tablecloth, doily or napkin, especially when using a heavy fabric on which a regular hem would be too bulky. Pull three or four threads at the desired width from the edge, leaving a solid fabric band as shown in Figure 33 a, then work hemstitch. Pull out the remaining threads to the edge, as shown in Figure 33 b. The corners have no fraying, as shown in Figure 33 c.

Fig. 33 a. *Fringing.*

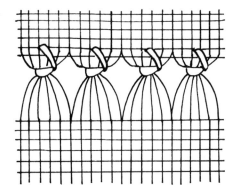

Fig. 33 b.

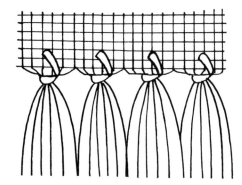

Fig. 33 c.

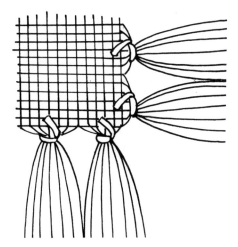

shapes of the design to the fabrics you are going to use. The threads of the appliqué fabric and those of the background fabric should always run in the same direction. Cut out the shape, leaving a ¼-inch (6-mm) seam allowance all around for a hem. Baste the hem. If the shape has curves, cut notches around the edge before hemming (Figure 34 a). Pin each appliqué piece over the appropriate outline on the background fabric. If appliqué shapes are going to overlap, place the largest pieces on the background first. The only exception to this rule are stems of flowers. The petals of the flower should cover the raw edge of the stem. Hold the appliqué to the fabric with basting stitches and then sew around the edges with blindstitches. Often decorative stitches are embroidered around the edges of appliqué shapes (Figure 34 b). When overcast or close buttonhole stitches are used, no hem is needed. Hold

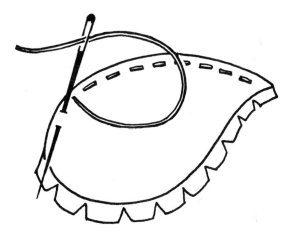

Fig. 34 a. *Appliqué Work.*

Fig. 34 b.

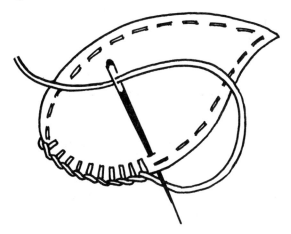

APPLIQUE (AW)

The term appliqué comes from the French. It means "to put on" and basically refers to the process of a fabric shape being applied onto a fabric background.

First transfer the entire design to the background fabric. Then transfer the various appliqués with basting stitches on outlines and then sew the shapes to the background with embroidery stitches, either by hand or machine, covering the basting stitches.

BEADED EMBROIDERY (BED)

Beads can be found in various sizes and shapes. They are made of materials such as glass, metal, wood and plastic and they come in an infinite range of colors, which results in the most beautiful effects.

Except for wood or chalk beads, beads are generally used for evening clothes and accessories. Their glitter is more in harmony with the rich fabrics used for this kind of garment. Beads are sewn with transparent nylon thread or with silk thread in a color to match the article being sewn.

There are two methods with which to sew on beads: a group of beads gathered and sewn on a single strand of thread is known as the "on string" method; or they can be attached singly with a short backstitch. The method to choose depends on the amount of space available.

Single Method

Bring the needle up at the required spot. String one bead and go down, making a stitch the size of the bead (Figure 35). Secure the bead with one backstitch underneath. Bring the needle up again one thread away and repeat with the next bead.

"On String" Method

To sew beads "on string" catch a number of beads on the needle and pull the thread through (Figure 36 a). With another needle and thread couch down beaded thread (Figure 36 b). Repeat for the next group of beads. Keep groups of beads even unless other instructions are given with the design.

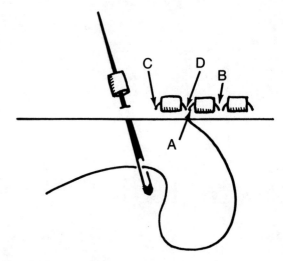

Fig. 35. *Single Method of Beading.*

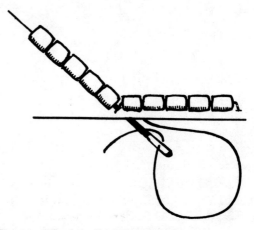

Fig. 36 a. *"On String" Method of Beading.*

Fig. 36 b.

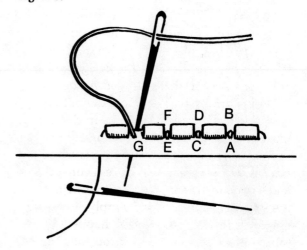

4. Working and finishing tips

THE FOLLOWING RULES and tips generally apply to all handwork embroidery and should be followed for best results.

- Press fabric before beginning work.
- Always put your work on a hoop, unless otherwise indicated in the instructions. If you are working on a fabric too small to be inserted in a hoop, hold your material in a convex position over your fingers. Another alternative is to sew the fabric to a larger piece and then put the whole piece in the hoop.
- Avoid pulling or puckering the work by making sure your needle is the right size.
- Try to cut lengths of thread that are neither too long nor too short for the designated area. Starting a new strand of thread in the middle of your work might become a difficult operation in some instances, such as in the case of hemstitching, or it may just be unsightly. You should, therefore, try to find places where starting a new thread will be less conspicuous and estimate thread lengths that will reach the destination. If you simply guess the length of the strand, it often happens that it turns out to be too short or too long. Before starting to work, cut two long strands of the same length and use one of them to work up to the specified spot. Then cut your thread

and cut off the excess. Measure the excess and cut that amount off the second thread. Keep that thread as a sample for cutting the lengths of the additional strands needed. This way you will always reach the designated spot without wasting your thread.

- Start stitches with a small knot on the back of the fabric, but end off stitches by making a few small backstitches in the nearest outline stitch or inside an area of the design that has not yet been embroidered (Figures 37 and 38). Bring the needle and thread to the front of the fabric and cut thread at the surface (Figure 39). This technique of ending off cuts down on the amount of knots. Knots can sometimes look messy and create a slight bulge in the embroidery.

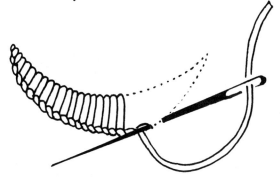

Fig. 37. *Ending off stitches in the nearest outline.*

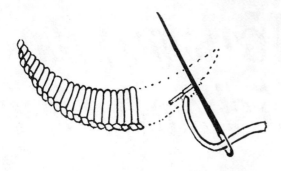

Fig. 38. *Ending off stitches in an unstitched area.*

Fig. 39. *Bringing the needle to the front and cutting thread.*

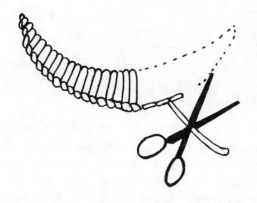

• For overlapping shapes, the ones that are underneath should be embroidered first.
• Do the inside areas of outlined shapes before outlines.

• When filling a shape make sure that stitches cover the area completely. Stitches must be adjusted sometimes to help corners, points and curves come out sharp and well defined. You may also have to "sneak in" a few small spot stitches here and there to keep things neat.
• The work should be kept clean and protected. But even when you have given meticulous care to your work, it can become soiled from handling. If your fabric is washable, soak it in warm water and mild soap. Do not squeeze or wring out and be sure to rinse out all soap. Roll work in a large terry cloth towel to remove the excess water. Then unroll the work and allow it to dry flat on a dry towel. Fabrics that can be dry-cleaned should be taken only to a good, reliable cleaner.
•When pressing the fabric, place fabric right side down on a well-padded ironing board and press on the wrong side. Your ironing board should be padded with two or three thick terry cloth towels. This is so the stitches won't be pressed flat. Wrap these towels across the top and secure them under the board with large safety or diaper pins. Always use a steam iron and place a press cloth between the iron and the fabric. Use a light, even touch. Press cottons and linens when they are damp and press silk when it is dry.

Part II

Hand Embroidery Projects

Crewel-embroidered
wool dress

Shown in color on page 33.

In this red wool dress, outline and filling stitches are combined for an interesting effect. All stitches are worked with beige wool yarn. This design could also be done on linen, but should not be done on a lightweight fabric.

Note: If you are making your own dress, finish sides and back seams according to pattern instructions before doing the embroidery. Add the lining after completing all embroidery.

THE MATERIALS

A simple red wool dress similar to the one illustrated (or pattern and fabric to make your own)
6 skeins DMC bulky embroidery wool in beige #7453

THE TOOLS

Equipment for enlarging and transferring the design, crewel or embroidery needle, tapestry needle, small scissors, embroidery hoop

THE DESIGN

1. Enlarge the design (Figure 40).
2. Transfer the enlarged design to the fabric, using the method suggested for wools in chapter 2.

THE EMBROIDERY

Put the work on the hoop and follow the stitching key.
1. Work all satin stitches, arrowheads, straight stitches, and lazy daisy stitches.
2. Next, work all stem stitch areas.
3. Work the close buttonhole areas.
4. Work French knots last.

THE FINISHING

Lightly press the embroidery with a steam iron on the wrong side of the fabric.

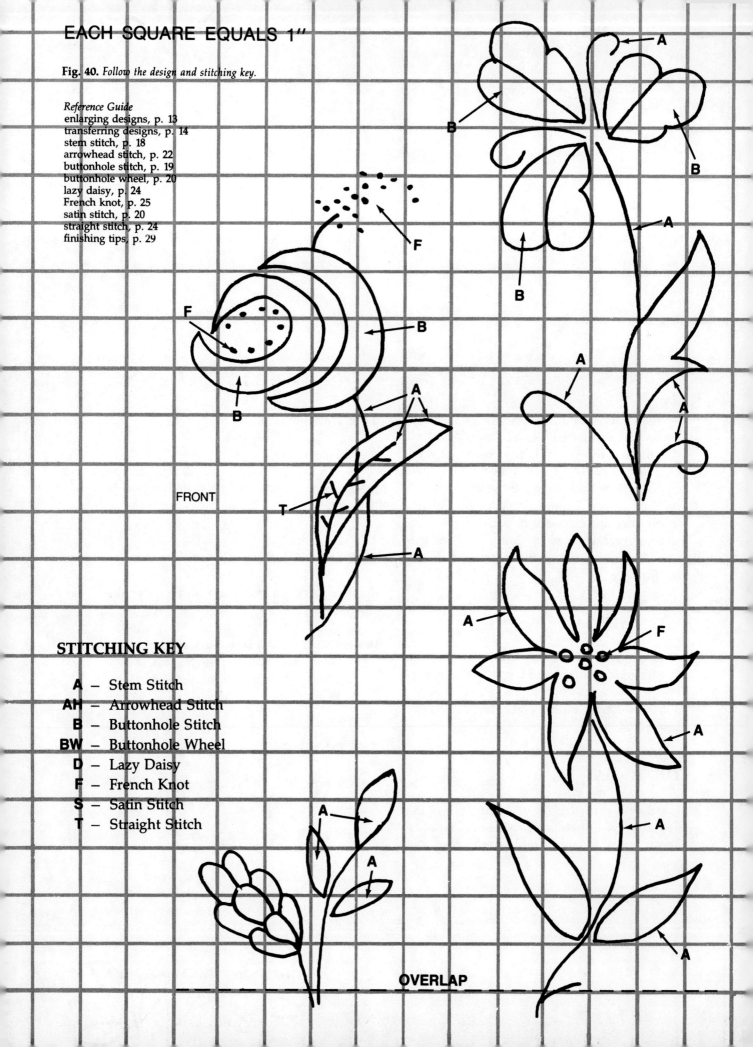

EACH SQUARE EQUALS 1"

Fig. 40. *Follow the design and stitching key.*

Reference Guide
enlarging designs, p. 13
transferring designs, p. 14
stem stitch, p. 18
arrowhead stitch, p. 22
buttonhole stitch, p. 19
buttonhole wheel, p. 20
lazy daisy, p. 24
French knot, p. 25
satin stitch, p. 20
straight stitch, p. 24
finishing tips, p. 29

FRONT

STITCHING KEY

A – Stem Stitch
AH – Arrowhead Stitch
B – Buttonhole Stitch
BW – Buttonhole Wheel
D – Lazy Daisy
F – French Knot
S – Satin Stitch
T – Straight Stitch

OVERLAP

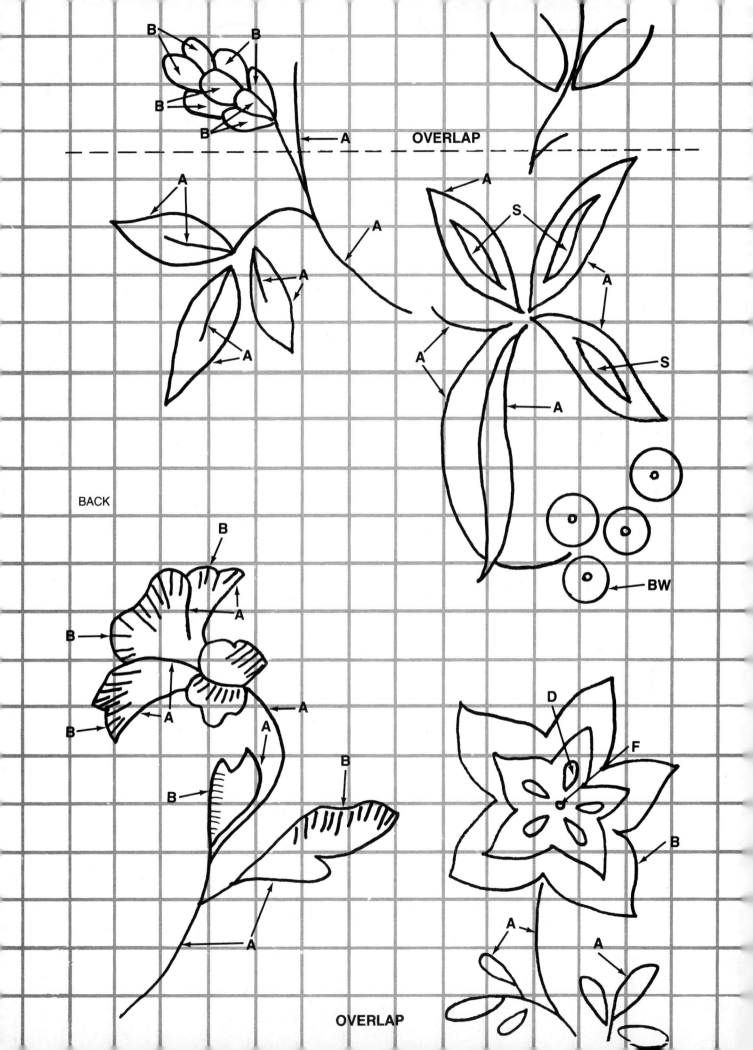

OVERLAP

BACK

OVERLAP

OVERLAP

BACK

AH

F

A

B

A

A

OVERLAP

EACH SQUARE EQUALS 1"

Folk-embroidered white blouse

Shown in color on page 34.

CENTRAL EUROPEAN folk embroidery was the inspiration for this design, which is used on collar and sleeves. It is suitable for light-weight or sheer fabrics such as organdy.

Note: If you are making your own blouse from a pattern, embroider the collar top before assembling the collar. Embroider the sleeves while flat, before seaming and attaching to the blouse.

THE MATERIALS

A plain white shirt or blouse with collar and full sleeves (or pattern and fabric to make your own)

11 skeins DMC 6-strand embroidery floss, 1 each of the following colors: poppy red #666, dark blue #796, light blue #518, dark green #911, light green #905, black #310, dark yellow #444, light yellow #742, light brown #922, orange #947 and violet #552

THE TOOLS

Equipment for enlarging and transferring the design, crewel or embroidery needle, small scissors, embroidery hoop

THE DESIGN

1. Enlarge the designs (Figure 41).
2. Transfer the enlarged designs to the fabric. The designs for collar and sleeves are shown only for the right sides. Remember to reverse the collar design ("flop" it from right to left) for the left side and simply repeat the right sleeve design for the left sleeve.

THE EMBROIDERY

Put the work on the hoop and follow the stitching key and color key. Use a double strand of floss throughout the work.

1. Work all satin stitch areas first.
2. Next, work all stem stitch areas, including the black outlines of the satin stitch motifs.
3. Work all French knots last.

THE FINISHING

Very lightly press the embroidery on the wrong side of the fabric using a steam iron.

EACH SQUARE EQUALS 1"

Fig. 41. *Follow the design and keys.*

Reference Guide
enlarging designs, p. 13
transferring designs, p. 14
satin stitch, p. 20
stem stitch, p. 18
French knot, p. 25
finishing tips, p. 29

STITCHING KEY

A – Stem Stitch
F – French Knot
S – Satin Stitch

COLOR KEY

1 – Poppy Red
2 – Dark Blue
3 – Light Blue
4 – Dark Green
5 – Light Green
6 – Black
7 – Dark Yellow
8 – Light Yellow
9 – Light Brown
10 – Orange
11 – Violet

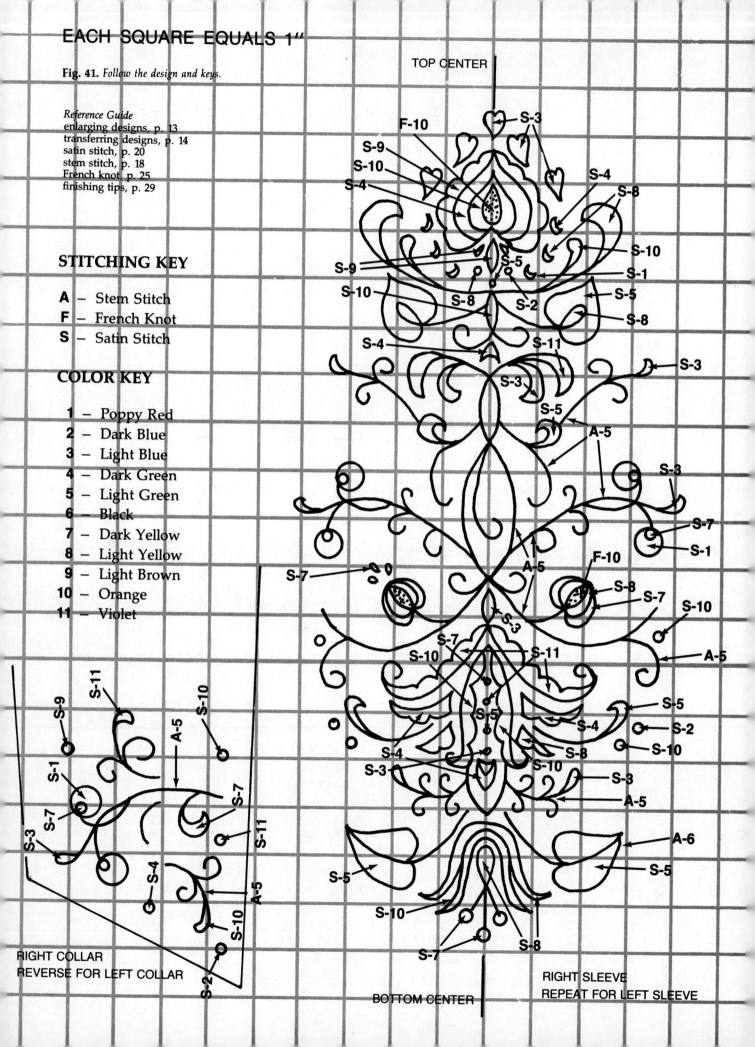

TOP CENTER

RIGHT COLLAR
REVERSE FOR LEFT COLLAR

BOTTOM CENTER

RIGHT SLEEVE
REPEAT FOR LEFT SLEEVE

Lace appliqué tablecloth

Shown in color on page 36.

This is the quickest project you could ever do. It is worked with lace appliqués cut out from "guipure" lace and sewn on the table-cloth. The sides of the tablecloth are done in long and short buttonhole stitches. This project is suitable for cotton and linen fabrics.

Note: The tablecloth pictured is 40 inches (100 cm) square. It required sixteen motifs for the center and one small flower for each corner. Adjust the number of motifs to the size of your own tablecloth.

THE MATERIALS

A red tablecloth in the size required for your table (or 1⅛ yards [1 m] of 45-inch [113-cm] red linen to make your own)
1 yard (95 cm) white "guipure" lace (more or less, depending on the size of your tablecloth)
basting thread
3 skeins mat-finish embroidery cotton twist in white
1 spool sewing thread in white

THE TOOLS

Small scissors, tape measure, dressmaker's chalk, length of string, sewing needle, crewel or embroidery needle, straight pins

THE DESIGN

Prepare the lace appliqués.

1. Cut the required number of appliqués for the center and one small flower for each corner from the lace piece (Figure 42). Use small embroidery scissors and cut neatly around each motif. Set aside.

2. Baste a 1-inch (2.5-cm) hem all around your tablecloth, mitering the corners. If your tablecloth already has a shorter or longer hem, rip it out and baste a 1-inch (2.5-cm) hem. Using dressmaker's chalk, mark a straight line all around the hem, 1 inch (2.5 cm) from the edge. This is your guideline for the buttonhole stitch.

3. Now measure and mark a circle in the center of the tablecloth to serve as a guide for placing the appliqués. To find the center, fold the cloth in half and then in half again. Press lightly with a steam iron to crease the quarter folds. Measure along the edge from center to hem and mark the midpoint with dress-maker's chalk. Open up the square. Attach dressmaker's chalk to string. Place chalk on the midpoint and, holding the string down firmly at the center, swing the chalk and make broken lines all around the circle (Figure 43). Run basting stitches all around the circle.

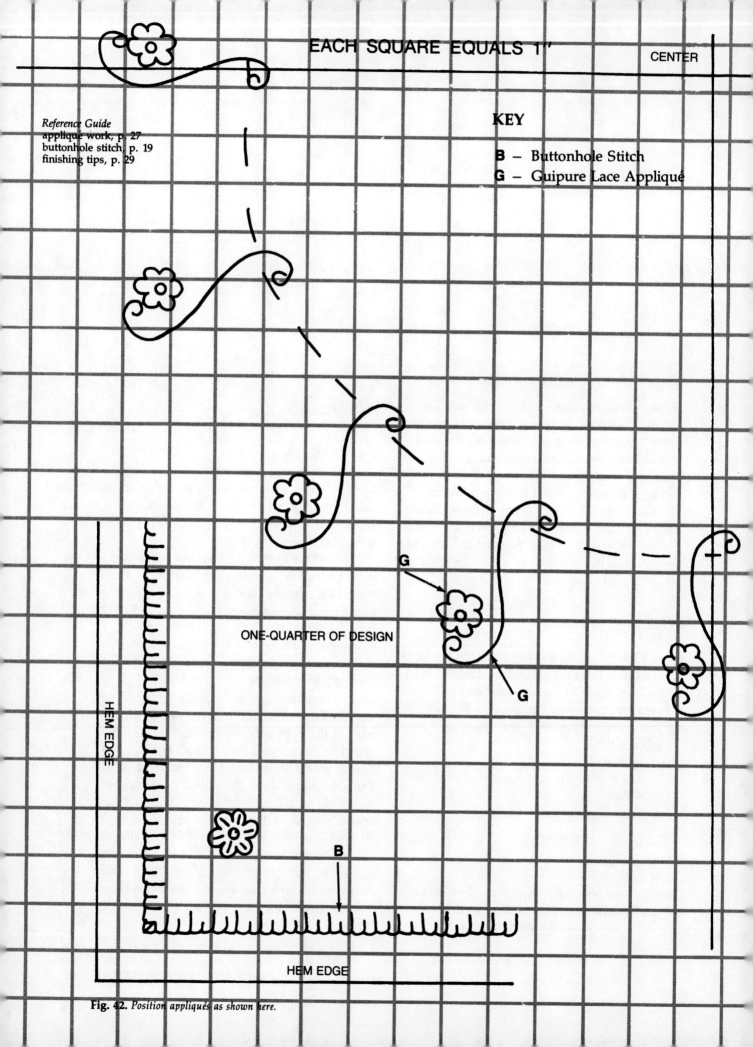

EACH SQUARE EQUALS 1"

CENTER

Reference Guide
appliqué work, p. 27
buttonhole stitch, p. 19
finishing tips, p. 29

KEY

B – Buttonhole Stitch
G – Guipure Lace Appliqué

ONE-QUARTER OF DESIGN

G

G

HEM EDGE

B

HEM EDGE

Fig. 42. *Position appliqués as shown here.*

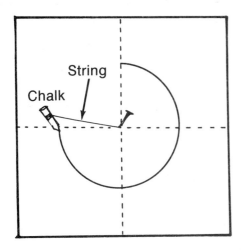

Fig. 43. *Drawing a circle with string and chalk.*

THE EMBROIDERY

1. Thread the embroidery or crewel needle with one strand of mat-finish embroidery cotton and start working the buttonhole stitching along the guideline near the hem (Figure 44). Alternate one long and one short

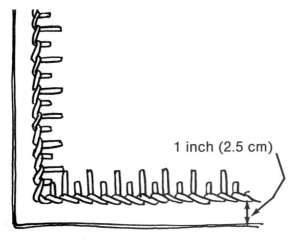

1 inch (2.5 cm)

Fig. 44. *Working the buttonhole stitching.*

stitch, leaving equal spaces between them as shown in the photograph, and catching the hem that has been folded and basted underneath. Work along all four sides.

2. Place your appliqué motifs around the basted circle, positioning one on each of the four pressed lines and distributing the others in between these four. Pin and baste each appliqué in place.

3. Sew the motifs to the tablecloth with small blindstitches.

4. Place a small flower motif on each corner of the tablecloth. Pin and baste in place.

5. Sew the motifs to the corners with small blindstitches.

THE FINISHING

1. Remove all basting stitches.

2. Using a well-padded board and a steam iron, lightly press the finished tablecloth on the wrong side. The dressmaker's chalk marks will come off with the use of a steam iron.

Note: If you have an oblong or oval tablecloth, you will probably want to place the center arrangement in an oval rather than a circle. To do this, start by folding the tablecloth in quarters and lightly pressing the fold lines as before. On each quarter and with dressmaker's chalk, mark the midpoint between center and hem on both long and short sides. Open up the tablecloth and connect these marks, making a freehand oval (Figure 45). Baste along the oval. Position appliqués on the basted line, placing one on each pressed line and evenly distributing the others. You'll find that you'll need more appliqués for an oval than for a circle. Pin, baste and then blindstitch in place. The corner appliqués and border are done the same way here as for a square tablecloth.

Fig. 45. *Making an oval.*

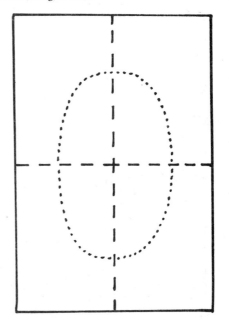

Hemstitched shirtdress

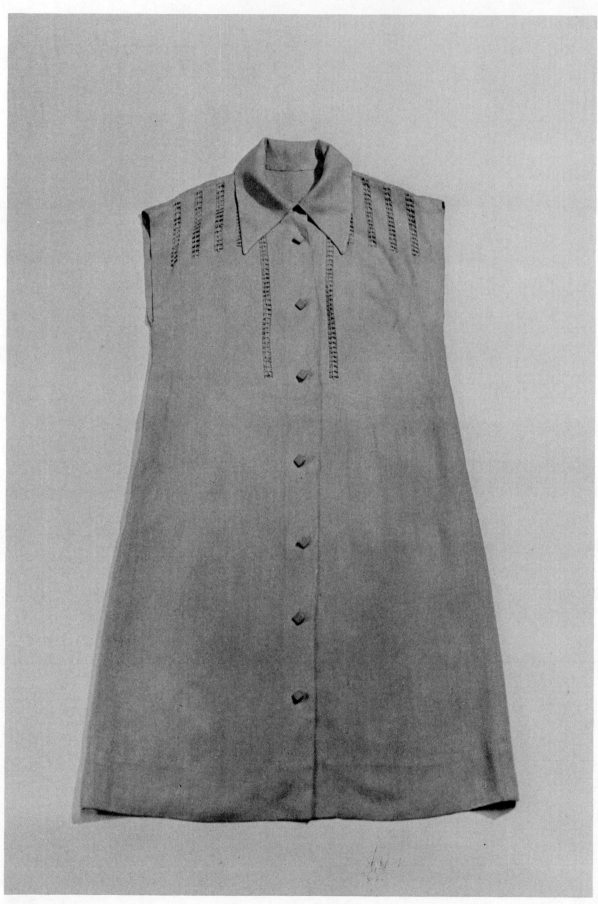

Shown in color on page 35.

HEMSTITCHING IS a very simple and easy way to decorate a plain linen shirtdress. The design is worked over an area where a number of vertical threads have been pulled.

Note: If you are making your own shirtdress, finish it according to the pattern directions before starting to embroider.

THE MATERIALS

A ready-made even-weave linen or similar fabric shirtdress (or pattern and fabric to make your own)
1 spool sewing thread in color to match dress
1 ball #5 pearl cotton in color to match dress

THE TOOLS

Tape measure, dressmaker's chalk, small scissors, straight pins, sewing needle, embroidery needle

THE DESIGN

1. Decide how you want to place hemstitching motifs. The exact design of the one shown in Figure 46 might have to be slightly altered according to the style of your own dress. With dressmaker's chalk, mark the length and width of the areas where threads are to be drawn. You might also mark the areas with basting stitches if you prefer.

2. Start pulling threads lengthwise. To do this, make a straight cut across the bottom of the area to be pulled with sharp scissors. In this case, it isn't necessary to cut across the top of the design area because this is the garment's seam allowance. However, if your design is placed in the center of the garment, both ends must be cut.

3. Using the point of the needle or a pin, very carefully pull out the first thread from one side and then the first thread from the opposite side (Figure 47). It is easiest to finish the area when threads are pulled from one side to the other. Finish pulling out all the threads in all the areas of the design.

Fig. 47. *Pulling out a thread.*

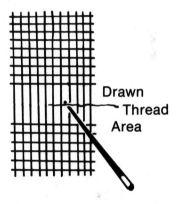

Drawn Thread Area

THE EMBROIDERY

1. Thread the sewing needle with sewing thread and work the ladder hemstitch along both edges of each drawn thread bar.

2. Thread the embroidery needle with the pearl cotton and start working the knotted stitch design along the center of the bar. Finish the knotted stitch design on all drawn thread bars.

THE FINISHING

With a steam iron set at the proper setting for the fabric, press work lightly on the wrong side.

Fig. 46. *Position of drawn thread bars.*

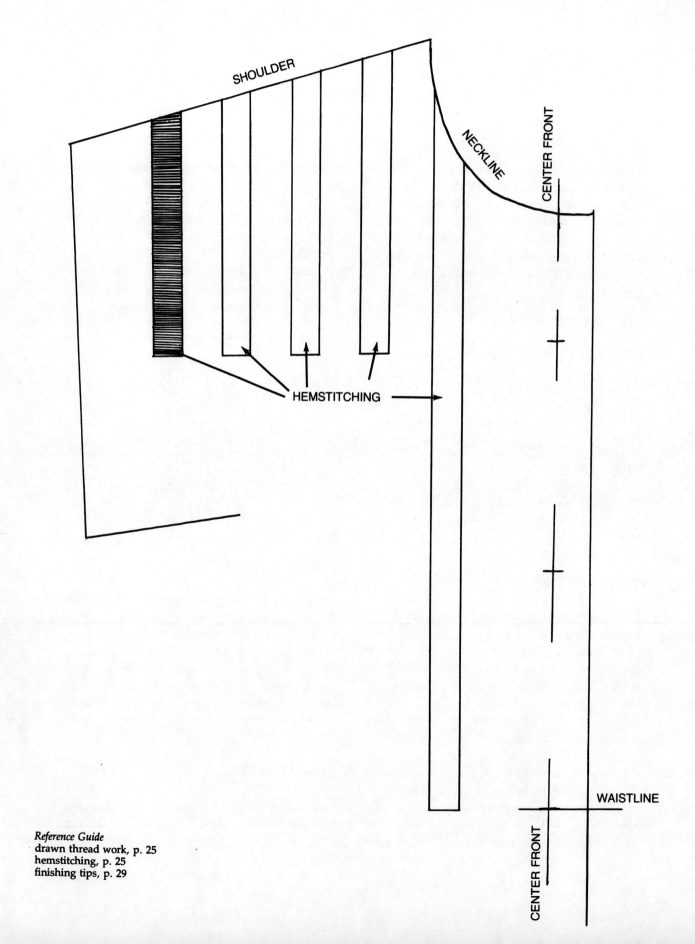

SHOULDER

NECKLINE

CENTER FRONT

HEMSTITCHING

WAISTLINE

CENTER FRONT

Cross-stitch
tea cloth

Shown in color on page 35.

This quick-and-easy project is worked in cross-stitch on even-weave fabric. Linen is the most suitable material for this design, which was inspired by rugs of North Africa.

THE MATERIALS

A ready-made square tablecloth approximately 32 inches square (or 1 yard [90 cm] brown even-weave linen to make your own)

1 yard 10-to-the-inch mesh canvas (if fabric is not even-weave)

8 skeins DMC #3 pearl cotton in blue #799

THE TOOLS

Crewel or embroidery needle, small scissors, embroidery hoop

THE PREPARATION

Baste the hem before embroidering. Turn hem ¼ inch (6 mm) in and baste. Then turn in 1 inch (2.5 cm) and baste again. With dressmaker's chalk, mark a guideline 1 inch (2.5 cm) from the edge all around.

THE DESIGN

The design chart should be followed as a guide (Figure 48). Each cross on the chart represents one stitch on the fabric. Only one symbol is used throughout because the design is worked in only one color. The chart represents one-quarter of the design. Follow it for the other three-quarters as well.

THE EMBROIDERY

1. If your fabric is not even-weave, use the 10-to-the-inch mesh canvas as your guide for counting threads. To do this, stitch the canvas to the top of the tablecloth with long basting stitches. Each stitch is made over two threads of the fabric, so there will be five cross-stitches to the inch. For even-weave fabrics, simply follow the chart and count the threads on your fabric.

2. Start working the cross-stitch design beginning with row 1 of the chart. When following the graph, work the second row as illustrated. Continue working from the chart until the design is completed. When cross-stitching the border guideline, catch the hem folded underneath.

THE FINISHING

1. If you used the canvas, remove basting stitches and begin pulling out the canvas threads, one by one (use tweezers, if necessary), until only the embroidery design remains on the tablecloth.

2. Lightly press the work on the wrong side of the fabric with a steam iron.

EACH SQUARE EQUALS 1''

Fig. 48. *Follow this design chart.*

Reference Guide
cross-stitch, p. 23
transferring designs, p. 14
finishing tips, p. 29

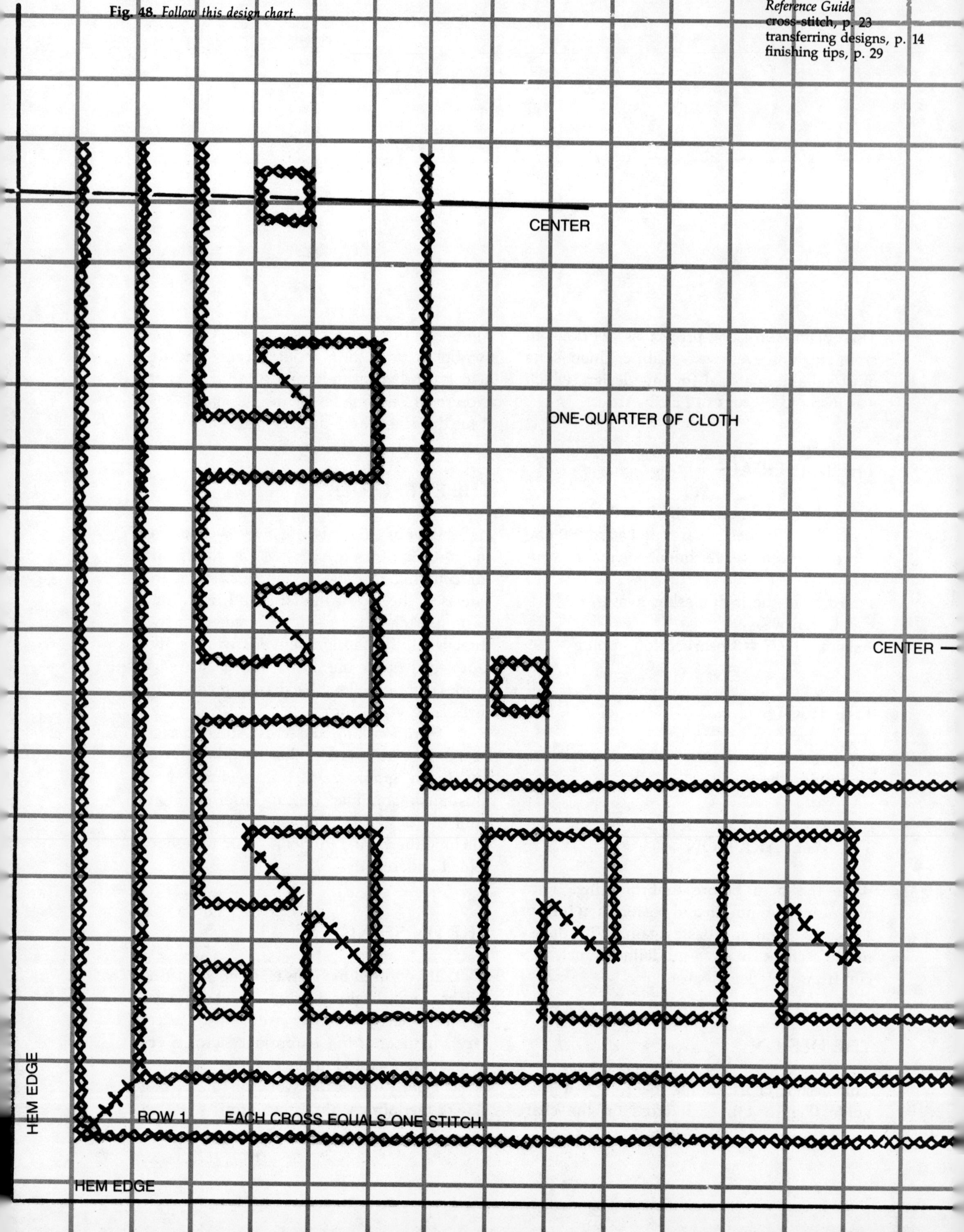
CENTER
ONE-QUARTER OF CLOTH
CENTER
HEM EDGE
ROW 1
EACH CROSS EQUALS ONE STITCH.
HEM EDGE

Wraparound Spanish blackwork skirt

Shown in color on page 36.

This design is an adaptation of fifteenth-century Spanish blackwork, although the technique used here has been much simplified. The thickness of the embroidery thread is an important element in blackwork, since it is this thickness that creates the impression of dark and light. The design is suitable for linen or wool.

Note: If you are making your own skirt, allow 1¼ inches (3 cm) at the top for casing and 2¼ inches (5.6 cm) at the bottom for the hem before cutting. At the side of the front and the bottom turn in ¼ inch (6 mm) and baste. Then turn in 2 inches (5 cm) and baste. The waistline casing will be done when the embroidery has been completed.

THE MATERIALS

A long white wraparound skirt similar to the one illustrated (or pattern and fabric to make your own)
DMC black #310 pearl cotton in the following quantities and sizes: 1 skein #8, 1 ball #5, 3 skeins #3 and 2 skeins #1
1 piece of elastic (enough for your waistline)
Velcro®, hook and eye, snaps or whatever you need to close the skirt at the side

THE TOOLS

Equipment for enlarging and transferring the design, crewel or embroidery needle, tapestry needle, small scissors, embroidery hoop

THE DESIGN

1. Enlarge the design (See Figure 49).
2. Transfer the enlarged design to the fabric, positioning it as shown in Figure 50.

THE EMBROIDERY

Put the work on the hoop and follow the design and keys.
1. First embroider the inside portions of the flowers and the leaves.
2. Next work all the outlines as indicated on the chart.

THE FINISHING

Note: If you are making your own skirt, finish by turning in casings and inserting elastic through. Attach Velcro® or closing device.

Lightly press the work on the wrong side with a steam iron.

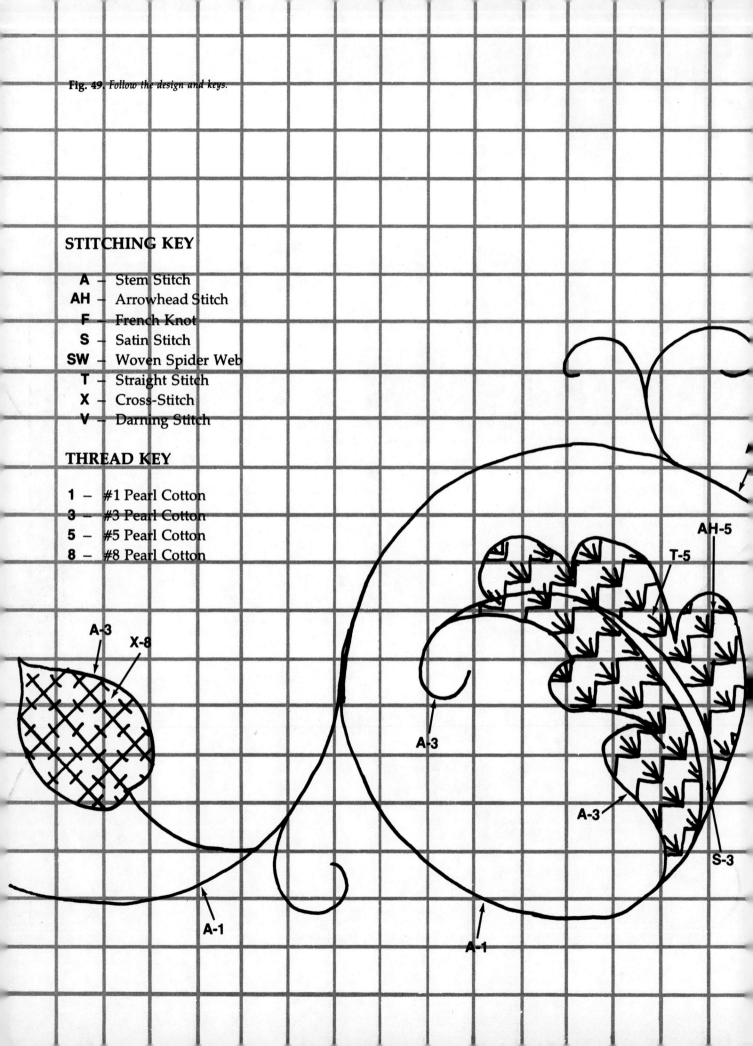

Fig. 49. *Follow the design and keys.*

STITCHING KEY

A	–	Stem Stitch
AH	–	Arrowhead Stitch
F	–	French Knot
S	–	Satin Stitch
SW	–	Woven Spider Web
T	–	Straight Stitch
X	–	Cross-Stitch
V	–	Darning Stitch

THREAD KEY

1	–	#1 Pearl Cotton
3	–	#3 Pearl Cotton
5	–	#5 Pearl Cotton
8	–	#8 Pearl Cotton

A-3

X-8

AH-5

T-5

A-3

A-3

S-3

A-1

A-1

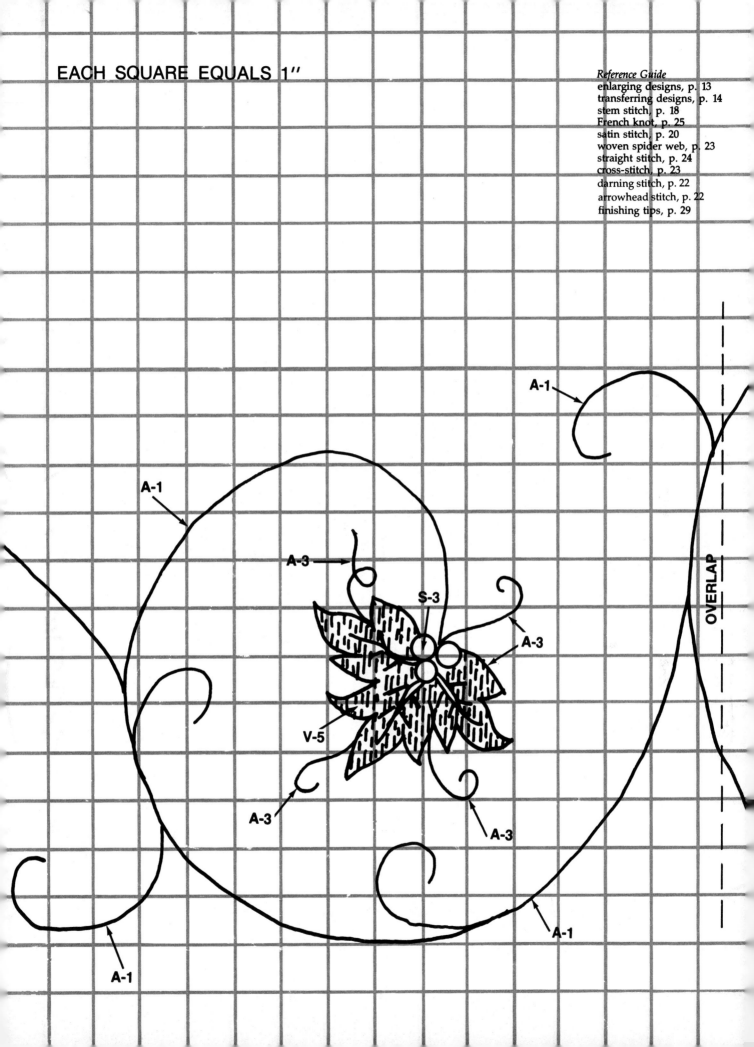

EACH SQUARE EQUALS 1"

A-1

A-1

A-3

S-3

A-3

V-5

A-3

A-3

A-1

A-1

OVERLAP

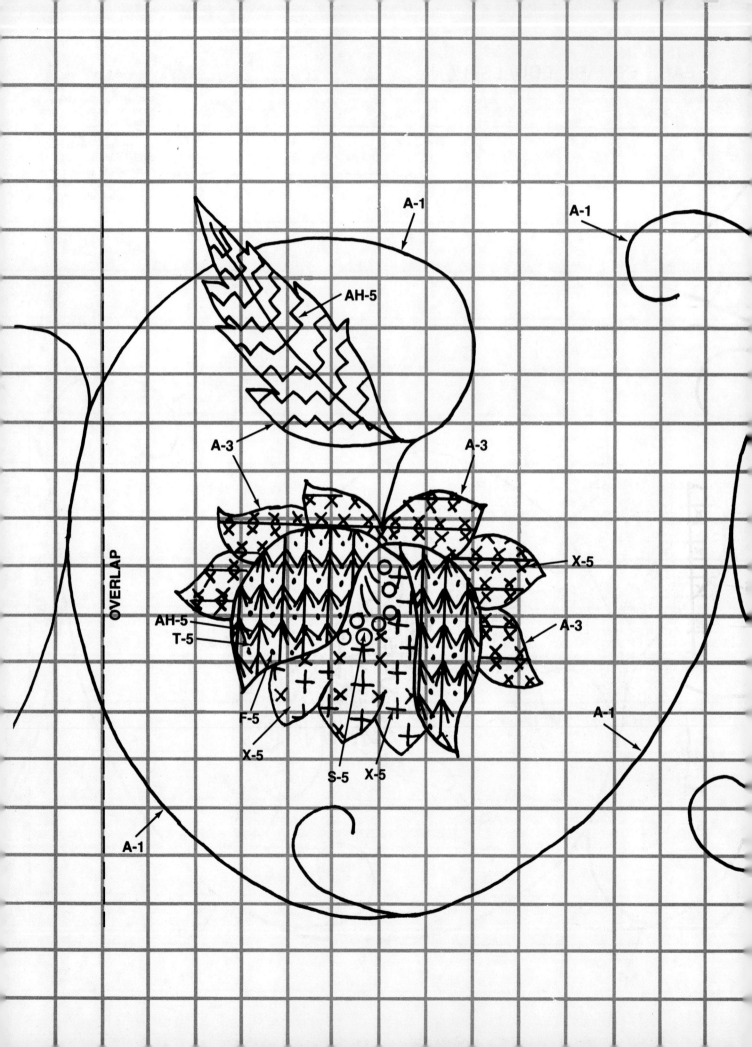

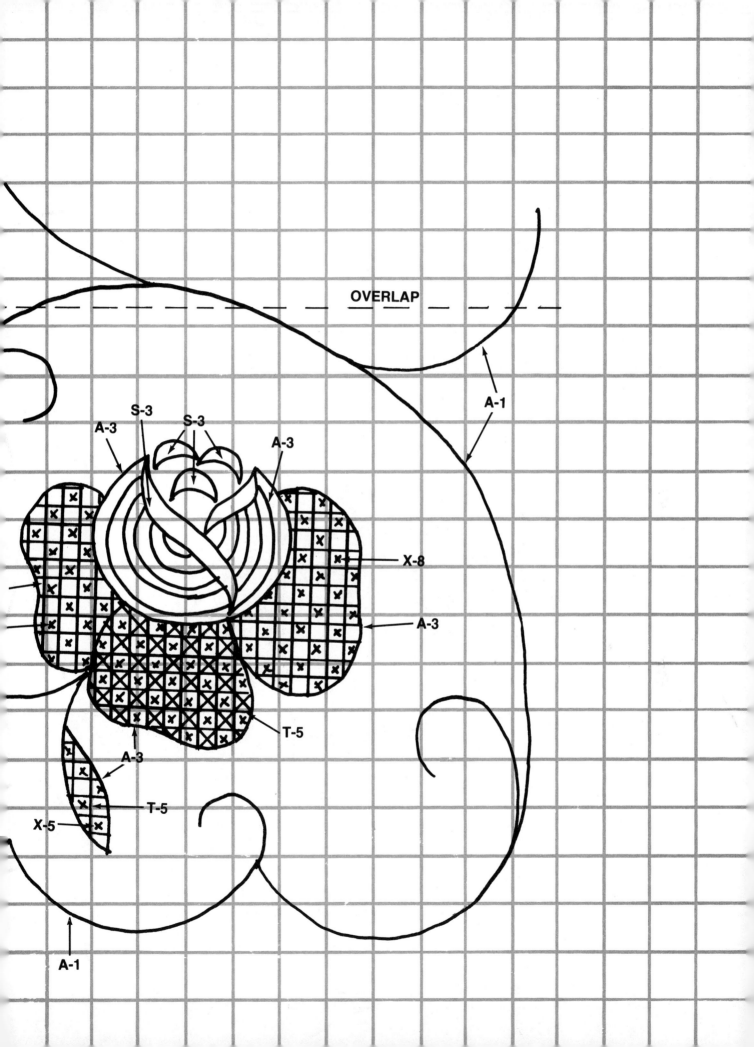

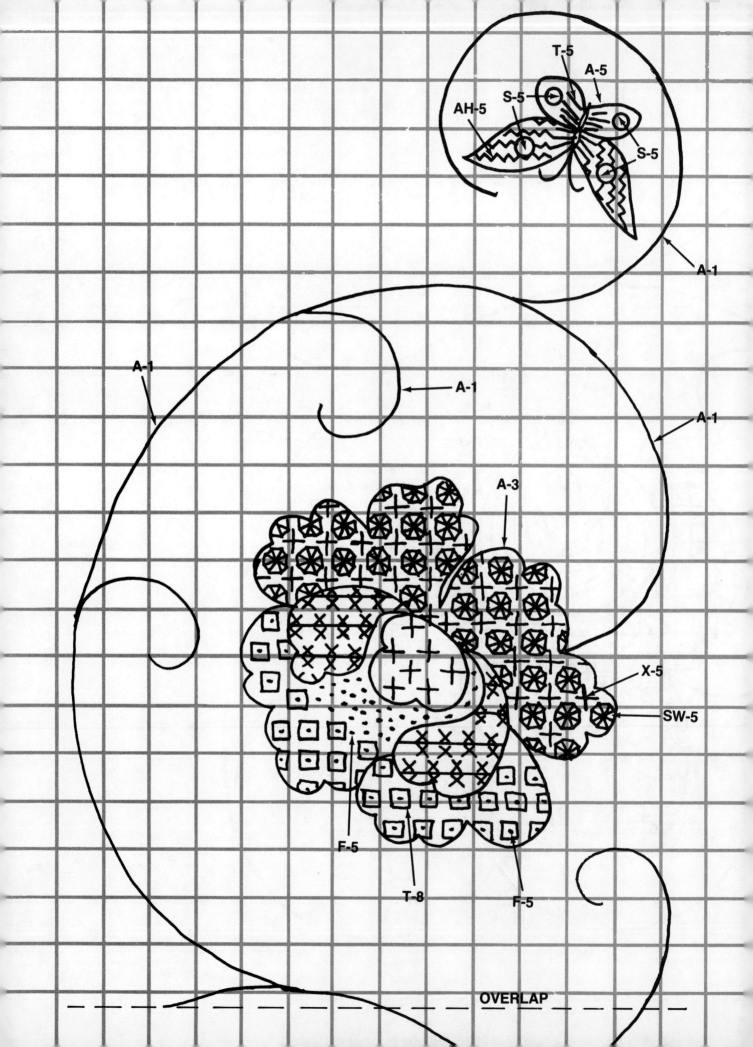

Fig. 50. *Positioning the design.*

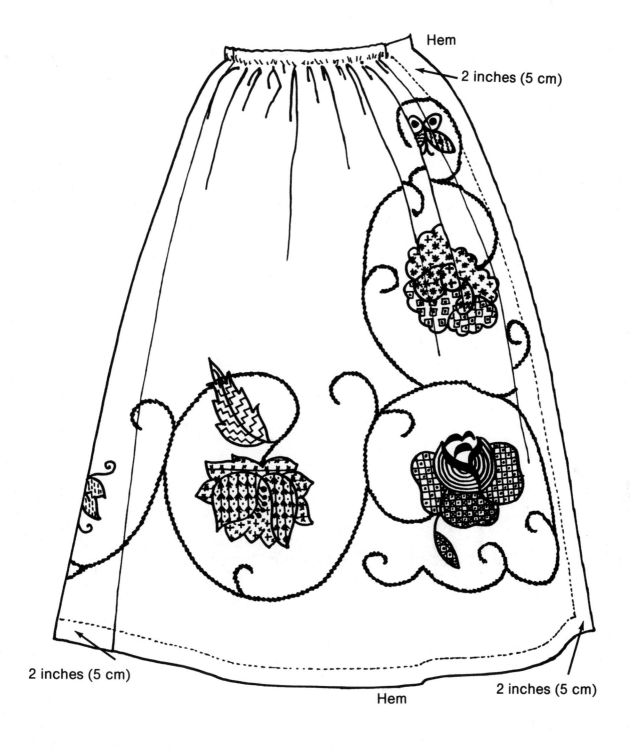

Hem

2 inches (5 cm)

2 inches (5 cm)

2 inches (5 cm)

Hem

Denim-look long T-dress

Shown in color on page 34.

Bold and beautiful embroidery in two shades of red adorns a knit T-dress. This design is also suitable for cotton, linen and wool.

THE MATERIALS

A blue denim cotton knit T-dress similar to the one illustrated (or fabric and pattern to make your own)

1 yard (90 cm) white organdy to line embroidered area

1 ball DMC #5 pearl cotton in red #309

1 ball DMC #5 pearl cotton in red #816

THE TOOLS

Equipment for enlarging and transferring the design, crewel or embroidery needle, tapestry needle, small scissors, embroidery hoop

THE DESIGN

1. Enlarge the design. (See Figure 51).
2. Transfer the design to the fabric.

THE EMBROIDERY

1. Baste the organdy on the wrong side of the dress, covering the area to be embroidered. Leave 1 inch (2.5 cm) all around the design. Be sure the organdy is very smooth over the fabric. This step will prevent the knit fabric from stretching out of shape and distorting the design.

2. Put the work on the hoop and follow the design and keys. Do the stitches in any order you like, but be sure embroidery stitches go through both layers of fabric. The trellis is done by stitching gridwork and then stitching a cross at the intersection of horizontal and vertical threads. Bring the needle up at point A, down at point B, up at C, down at D and so on until the grid is completed. Start at point M for the crosses (Figure 52).

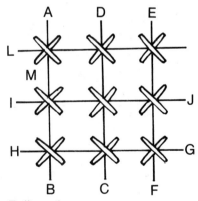

Fig. 52. *Trellis work.*

THE FINISHING

1. When the embroidery is finished, remove the basting stitches from the organdy. Trim organdy, leaving 1 inch (2.5 cm) above and below the embroidery.

2. Lightly press work on the wrong side of the fabric with a steam iron.

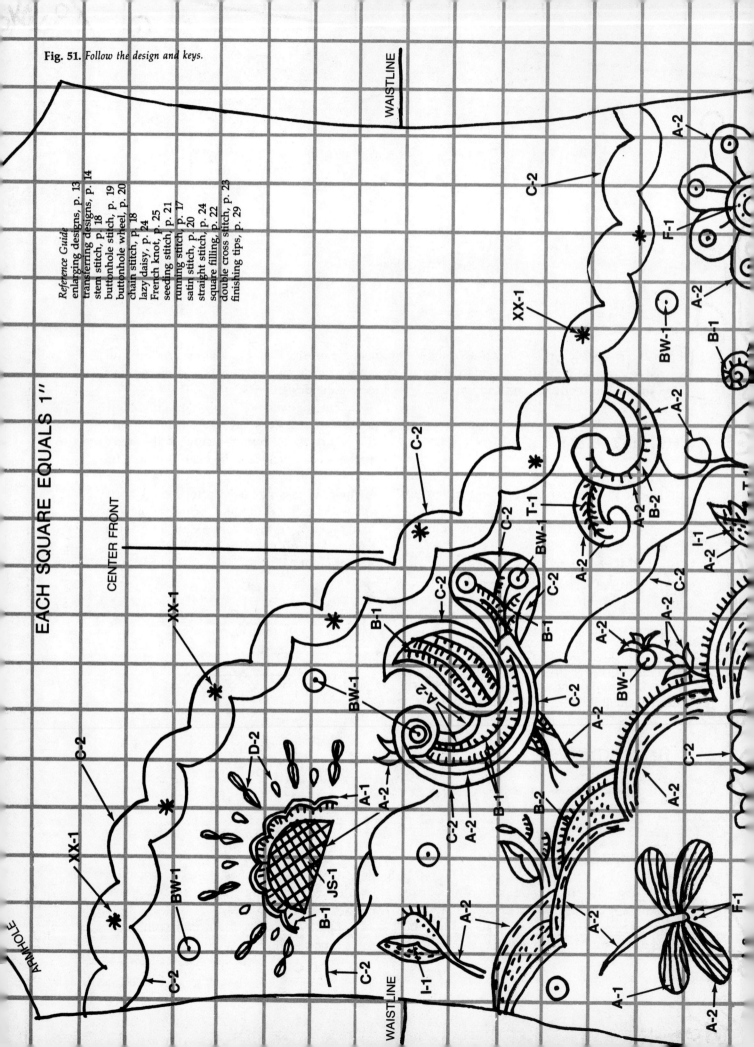

Fig. 51. *Follow the design and keys.*

EACH SQUARE EQUALS 1"

Reference Guide
enlarging designs, p. 13
transferring designs, p. 14
stem stitch, p. 18
buttonhole stitch, p. 19
buttonhole wheel, p. 20
chain stitch, p. 18
lazy daisy, p. 24
French knot, p. 25
seeding stitch, p. 21
running stitch, p. 17
satin stitch, p. 20
straight stitch, p. 24
square filling, p. 22
double cross stitch, p. 23
finishing tips, p. 29

WAISTLINE

CENTER FRONT

ARMHOLE

WAISTLINE

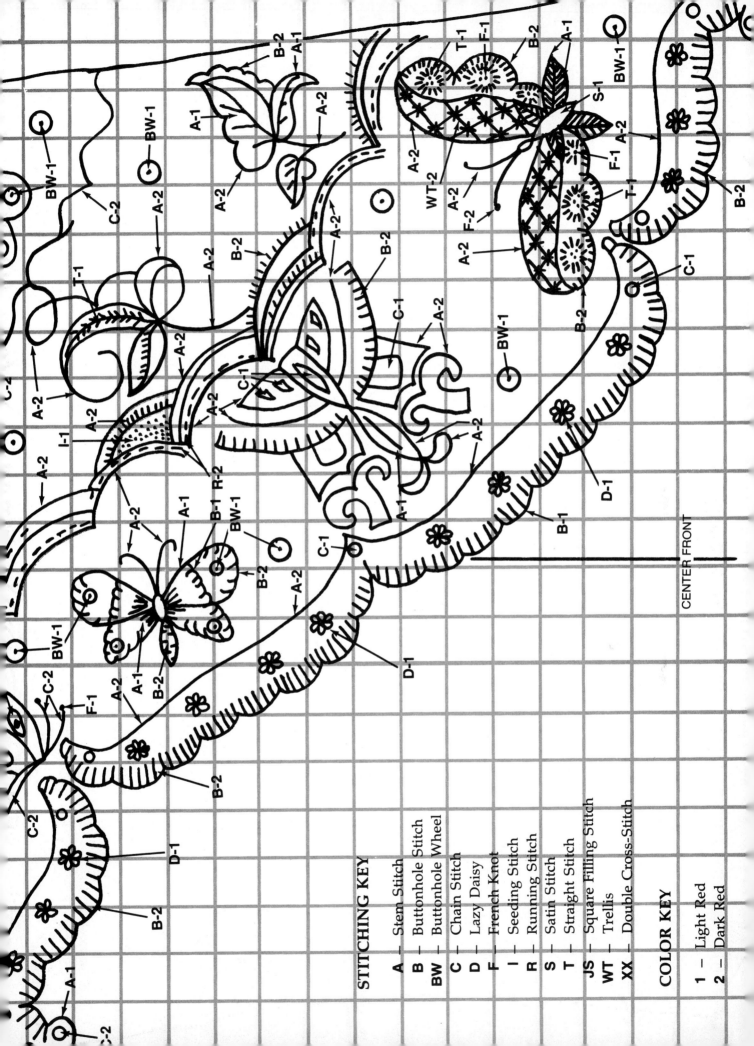

STITCHING KEY

A – Stem Stitch
B – Buttonhole Stitch
BW – Buttonhole Wheel
C – Chain Stitch
D – Lazy Daisy
F – French Knot
I – Seeding Stitch
R – Running Stitch
S – Satin Stitch
T – Straight Stitch
JS – Square Filling Stitch
WT – Trellis
XX – Double Cross-Stitch

COLOR KEY

1 – Light Red
2 – Dark Red

CENTER FRONT

Gray tablecloth
with pink embroidery

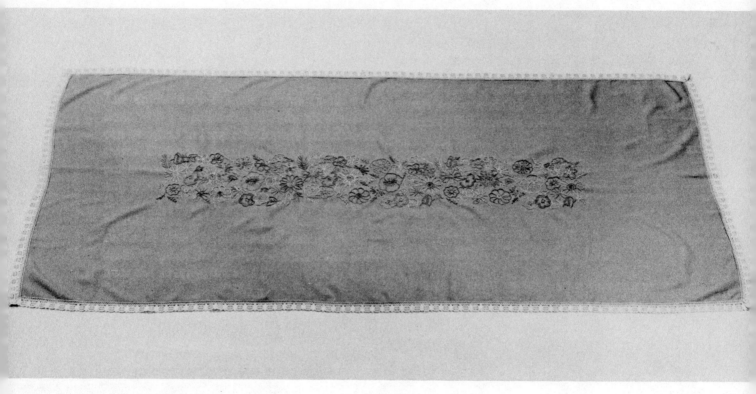

Shown in color on page 33.

Four SHADES of pink are used for the attractive and modern design on this gray linen tablecloth.

THE MATERIALS

A ready-made tablecloth, 2 yards (approximately 2 m) long (or 2⅛ yards [about 2 m] of gray linen to make your own)

4½ yards (4.15 m) of 1¼-inch- (3.2-cm-) wide pink lace edging

8 balls DMC #5 pearl cotton, 2 balls each in the following colors: pink #335, pink #776, pink #889 and pink #3326

THE TOOLS

Equipment for enlarging and transferring the design, dressmaker's chalk, crewel or embroidery needle, small scissors, embroidery hoop

THE PREPARATION

If you are making your own tablecloth, turn in ¼ inch (6 mm) twice for the hem all around and baste. For a ready-made tablecloth, rip out the existing hem and baste in this manner.

THE DESIGN

Note: One-third of the design is given in the drawing. Repeat twice for the complete design.

1. Enlarge the design (Figure 53).
2. Transfer the enlarged design to the fabric, repeating the design twice.

THE EMBROIDERY

Put the work on the hoop and follow the keys. Vary the shades of pink according to taste.

1. Work all stem stitch areas first.
2. Next, work all straight stitch areas.
3. Buttonhole stitch areas are worked next.
4. Now, complete all lazy daisy stitches.
5. Next, do all the French knots.
6. Attach the lace edging to the tablecloth using a closed buttonhole stitch. Miter the corners.

THE FINISHING

Lightly press work on the wrong side of the fabric with a steam iron.

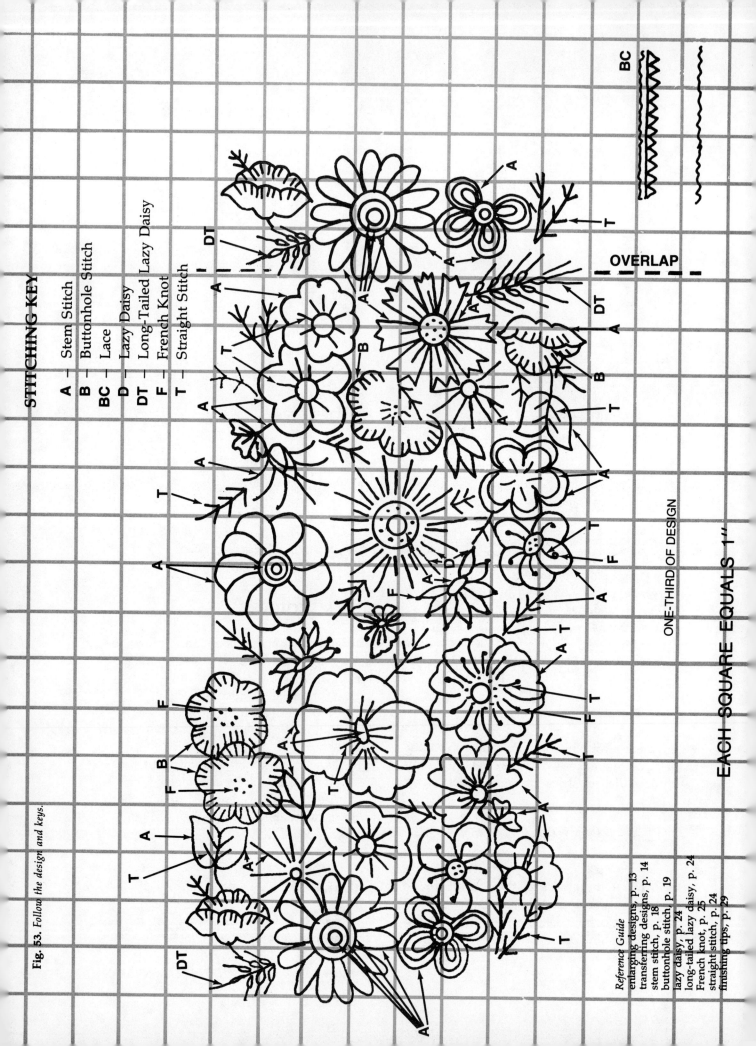

Fig. 53. Follow the design and keys.

STITCHING KEY

A — Stem Stitch
B — Buttonhole Stitch
BC — Lace
D — Lazy Daisy
DT — Long-Tailed Lazy Daisy
F — French Knot
T — Straight Stitch

OVERLAP

ONE-THIRD OF DESIGN

EACH SQUARE EQUALS 1"

Reference Guide
enlarging designs, p. 13
transferring designs, p. 14
stem stitch, p. 18
buttonhole stitch, p. 19

lazy daisy, p. 24
long-tailed lazy daisy, p. 24
French knot, p. 25
straight stitch, p. 24
finishing tips, p. 29

Sprays of leaves tablecloth

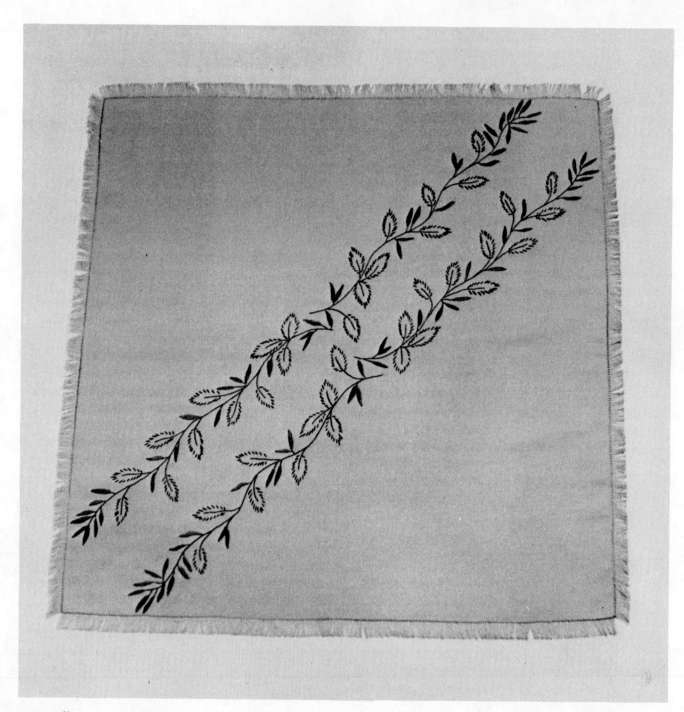

Shown in color on page 35.

Long sprays of leaves make this project a true "quickie." The design is suitable for linen, cotton or velvet fabrics.

Note: If you are making your own tablecloth, don't finish the edges until you have finished the embroidery.

THE MATERIALS

A ready-made orange linen tablecloth, 1 square yard (1 sq. m) (or 1⅛ yards [about 1 m] orange linen to make your own)

DMC 6-strand embroidery floss, 2 skeins each of the following colors: green #911, green #907, green #701

1 ball DMC #8 pearl cotton in variegated green #99 for hemstitching

THE TOOLS

Equipment for enlarging and transferring the design, dressmaker's chalk, crewel or embroidery needle, small scissors, embroidery hoop

THE DESIGN

Note: The design can be adjusted to larger or smaller tablecloths by adding or subtracting sprays.

1. Enlarge the design (See Figure 54).

2. Transfer the enlarged design to the fabric, following Figure 55 for placement. Draw a line with dressmaker's chalk across the diagonal of the fabric to serve as a guide.

THE EMBROIDERY

Put the work on the hoop and follow the keys. Work with three strands of thread throughout.

1. Work stem stitch areas first.

2. Next, work straight stitch areas.

3. Work close buttonhole stitch areas last, skipping two threads in between each stitch.

4. Cut off the hemline of your ready-made tablecloth. Prepare the edges for fringing.

5. Using the shaded green pearl cotton, work hemstitching along the top edge of the fringing with one strand of thread.

THE FINISHING

Lightly press work on the wrong side of the fabric with a steam iron.

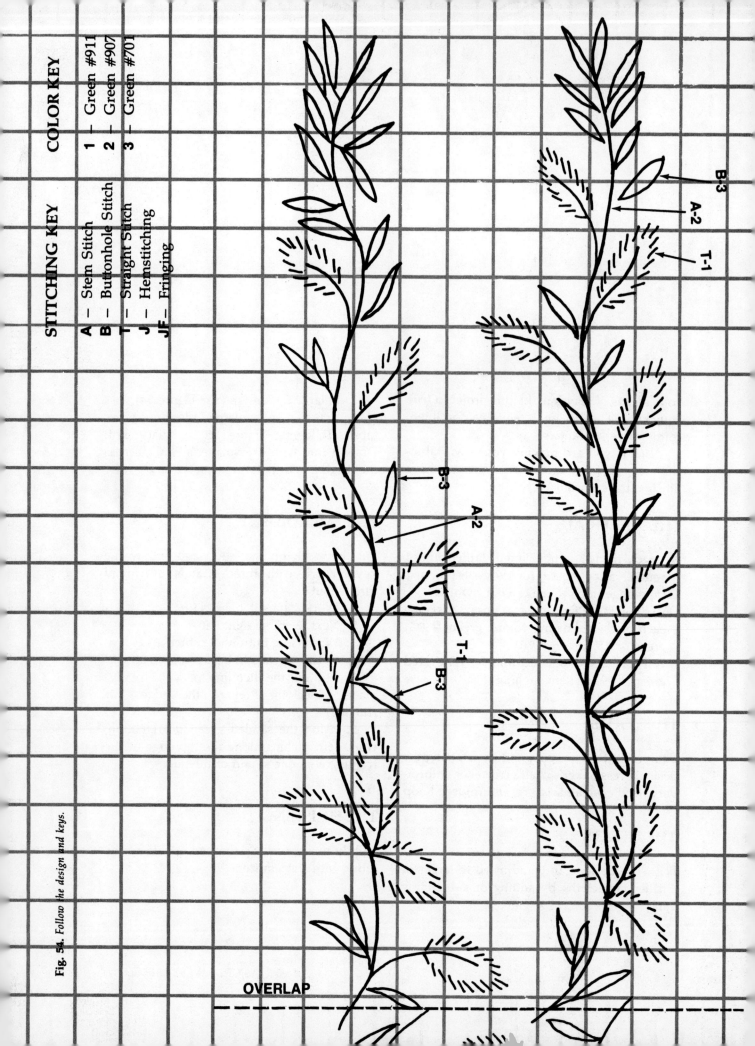

COLOR KEY

1 – Green #911
2 – Green #907
3 – Green #701

STITCHING KEY

A – Stem Stitch
B – Buttonhole Stitch
T – Straight Stitch
J – Hemstitching
JF – Fringing

Fig. 54. Follow the design and keys.

B-3
A-2
T-1

B-3
A-2

T-1
B-3

OVERLAP

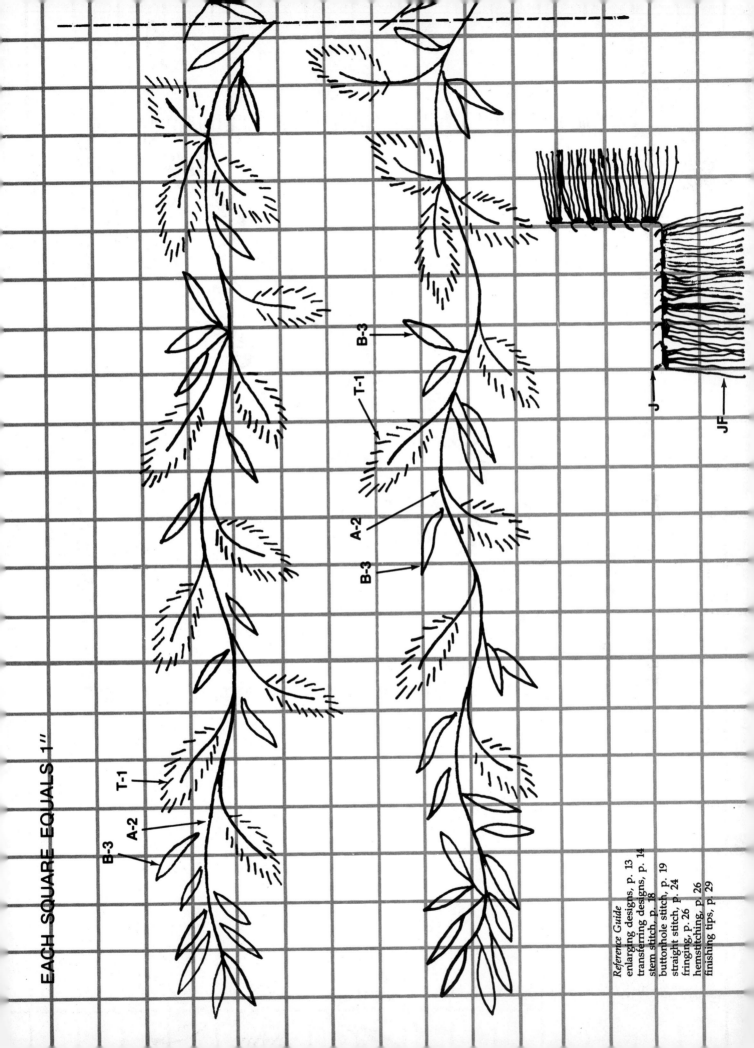

EACH SQUARE EQUALS 1"

B-3
A-2
T-1

B-3
A-2
T-1

B-3
T-1
A-2
B-3

J
JF

Reference Guide
enlarging designs, p. 13
transferring designs, p. 14
stem stitch, p. 18
buttonhole stitch, p. 19
straight stitch, p. 24
fringing, p. 26
hemstitching, p. 26
finishing tips, p. 29

Fig. 55. *Positioning the design.*

Bare-shouldered evening dress

Shown in color on page 34.

A CLASSIC BLACK evening dress is given a touch of luxury with a beautiful multicolored embroidery design. It is suitable for medium-to-lightweight fabrics such as crepe, satin, linen and wool. The dress shown here is made of black satin crepe.

Note: If you are making your own dress, embroider it before finishing.

THE MATERIALS

A plain black dress similar to the one illustrated (or pattern and fabric to make your own)

8 spools silk buttonhole twist, 1 each of the following colors: white, red, pink, shocking pink, yellow, emerald green, blue, gold

1 spool DMC Article #280 metallic gold thread

1 piece of elastic (enough for your waistline)

THE TOOLS

Equipment for enlarging and transferring the design, dressmaker's chalk, crewel or embroidery needle, small scissors, embroidery hoop

THE DESIGN

1. Enlarge the design (See Figure 56).

2. Transfer the enlarged design to the fabric. The design should begin 1½ inches (3.75 cm) up from the waistline. With dressmaker's chalk, mark the center and waistline of the dress front to serve as a guide.

THE EMBROIDERY

Place the work on the hoop and follow the stitching key.

1. Work all the large shapes (butterflies and body of bird) first. Do the satin stitches to fill the butterflies before you do the small dots and gold stripes on their wings and bodies.

2. Next, finish all the smaller shapes, such as dots, hearts, stems and S-shapes.

THE FINISHING

Note: If you are making your own dress, finish it according to pattern directions.

When the embroidery is finished, lightly press it on the wrong side of the fabric with a steam iron.

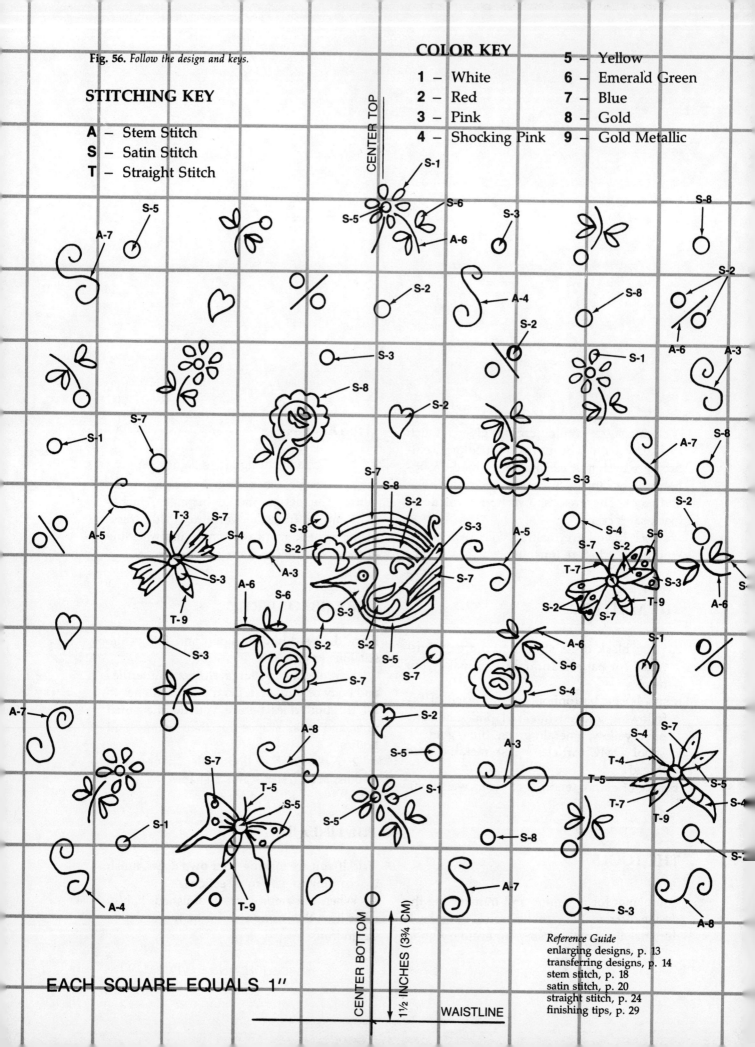

Fig. 56. *Follow the design and keys.*

STITCHING KEY

A – Stem Stitch
S – Satin Stitch
T – Straight Stitch

COLOR KEY

1 – White		**5** – Yellow
2 – Red		**6** – Emerald Green
3 – Pink		**7** – Blue
4 – Shocking Pink		**8** – Gold
		9 – Gold Metallic

CENTER TOP

CENTER BOTTOM

1½ INCHES (3¾ CM)

WAISTLINE

EACH SQUARE EQUALS 1"

Reference Guide
enlarging designs, p. 13
transferring designs, p. 14
stem stitch, p. 18
satin stitch, p. 20
straight stitch, p. 24
finishing tips, p. 29

Floral table runners

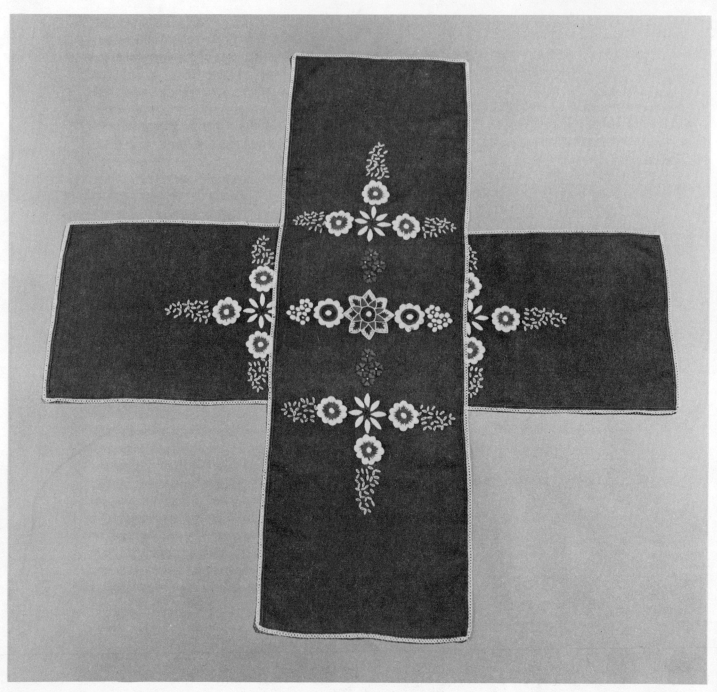

Shown in color on page 33.

These two linen runners, crossing each other at right angles, make an unusual table cover for informal meals. This design is suitable for linen and cotton.

THE MATERIALS

2 yards (about 2 m) royal blue linen
9 yards (about 9 m) white edging trim
26 skeins DMC Article #89 mat-finish cotton embroidery twist, 13 skeins each in white and red #2304

THE TOOLS

Equipment for enlarging and transferring the design, crewel or embroidery needle, small scissors, embroidery hoop

THE PREPARATION

1. Measure and cut two rectangles 57 by 21 inches (142.5 by 52.5 cm).
2. Turn in a ¼-inch (6-mm) hem twice. Baste. The hem will be finished later with a stem stitch, which will also be used to attach the edging.
3. Fold the runners in half and run a line of basting stitches from end to end to mark the center. This will aid you in positioning the design.

THE DESIGN

1. Enlarge the design (See Figure 57).
2. Transfer the enlarged design to one of your rectangles, placing it as shown in Figure 58. This will be the top runner.
3. For the lower runner transfer the design, omitting the central motif but allowing for the space.

THE EMBROIDERY

Put the work on the hoop and follow the keys.

1. Proceed with embroidery in any order you like, but remember that filling stitches should be done before outlines.
2. For the grouping of petals at the ends, work a lazy daisy stitch in white for each and fill in the center with a straight stitch in red.
3. Baste the edging trim to the hem and attach it with stem stitches, using red embroidery cotton (See Figure 59).

THE FINISHING

1. Remove all basting stitches.
2. Lightly press work on the wrong side with a steam iron.

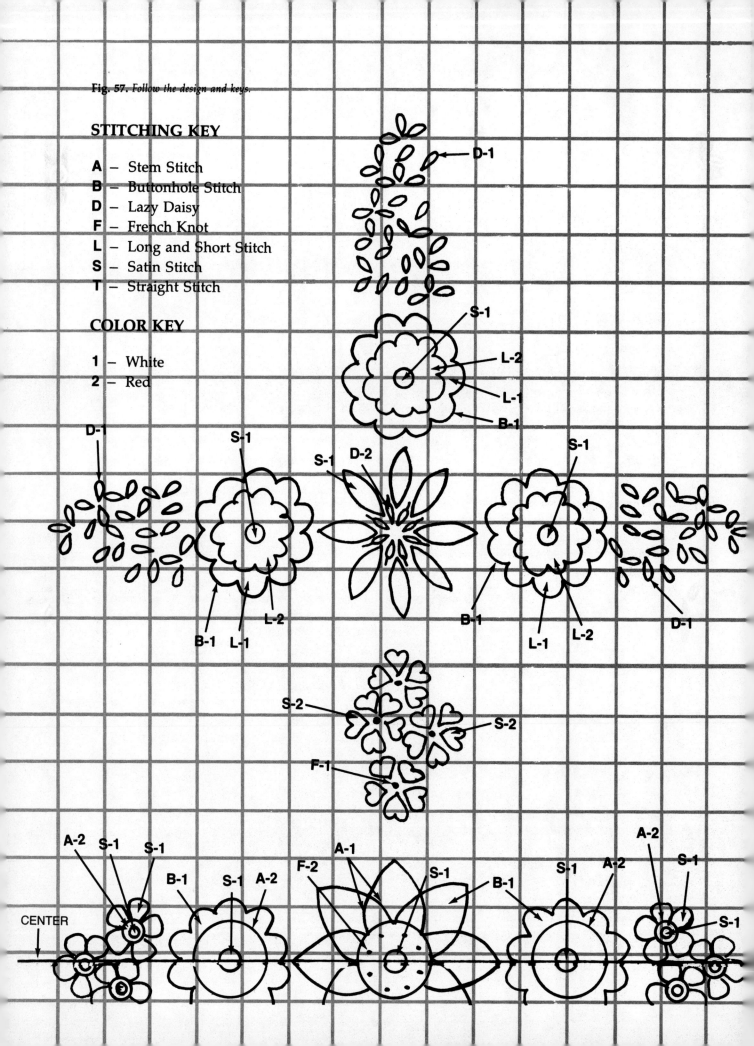

Fig. 57. *Follow the design and keys.*

STITCHING KEY

A – Stem Stitch
B – Buttonhole Stitch
D – Lazy Daisy
F – French Knot
L – Long and Short Stitch
S – Satin Stitch
T – Straight Stitch

COLOR KEY

1 – White
2 – Red

D-1

S-1
L-2
L-1
B-1

D-1

S-1

S-1   D-2

S-1

D-1

B-1   L-1

L-2

B-1

L-1   L-2

D-1

S-2

S-2

F-1

A-2 S-1   S-1

B-1

S-1   A-2

F-2   A-1

S-1

B-1

S-1   A-2

A-2

S-1

CENTER

S-1

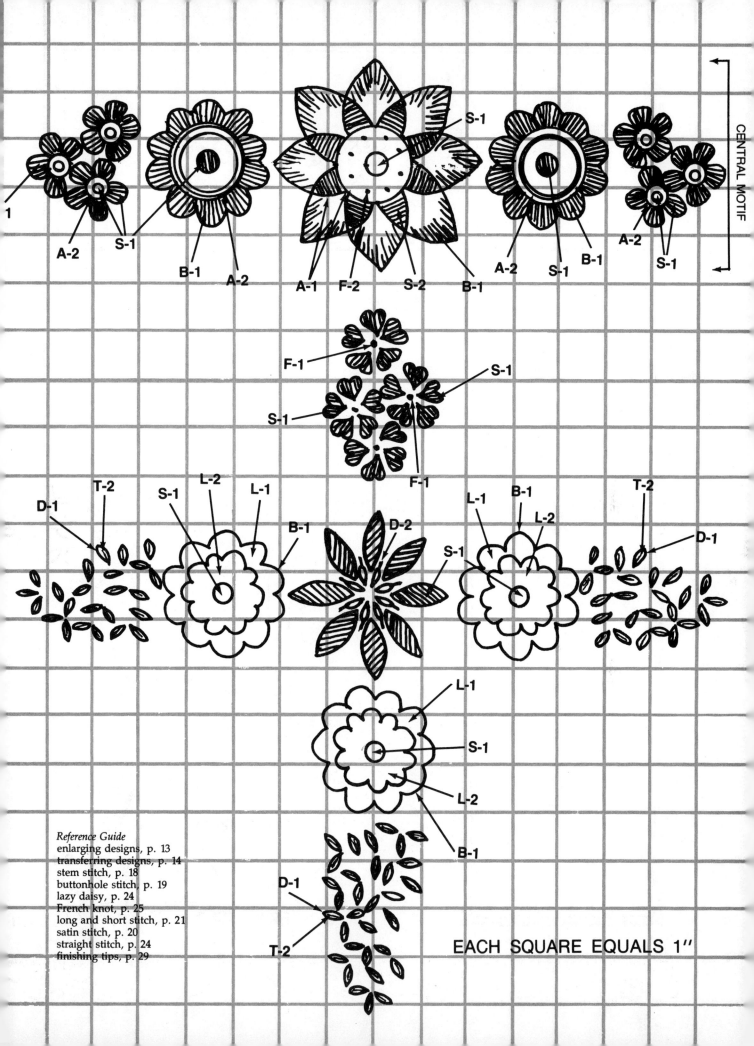

1

A-2

S-1

B-1

A-2

A-1 F-2 S-2 B-1

S-1

A-2 S-1 B-1

A-2

S-1

F-1

S-1

S-1

F-1

D-1 T-2 S-1 L-2 L-1

B-1

D-2

L-1 B-1 L-2

T-2 D-1

S-1

L-1

S-1

L-2

B-1

D-1

T-2

Reference Guide
enlarging designs, p. 13
transferring designs, p. 14
stem stitch, p. 18
buttonhole stitch, p. 19
lazy daisy, p. 24
French knot, p. 25
long and short stitch, p. 21
satin stitch, p. 20
straight stitch, p. 24
finishing tips, p. 29

EACH SQUARE EQUALS 1"

Top Runner

Fig. 58. *Positioning the design.*

Bottom Runner

Fig. 59. *Attaching the edging.*

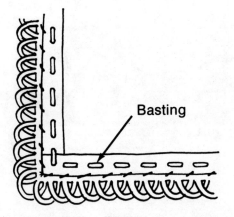

Basting

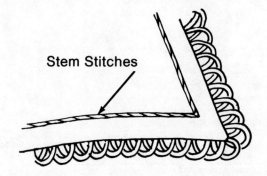

Stem Stitches

Beaded cocktail dress

Shown in color on page 33.

THIS DESIGN can be easily adapted for a long dress, although the short version is shown here. The dress in the photograph is made of silk taffeta, but other suitable materials are worsted wool and faille.

THE MATERIALS

A silk taffeta dress similar to the one illustrated (or pattern and fabric to make your own)

½ pound (¼ kilogram) antique gold beads

1 spool invisible nylon thread or gold-color sewing thread

THE TOOLS

Equipment for enlarging and transferring the design, small scissors, crewel or embroidery needle, embroidery hoop

THE DESIGN

1. Enlarge the design (See Figure 60).
2. Transfer the enlarged design.

THE EMBROIDERY

Put the work on the hoop and follow the stitching key.

1. The single method of bead embroidery should be used throughout most of the design. Work these areas first.

2. Work areas "on string" wherever you can and if you wish.

THE FINISHING

Lightly press work on the wrong side of the fabric with a steam iron, being careful not to crush the beads.

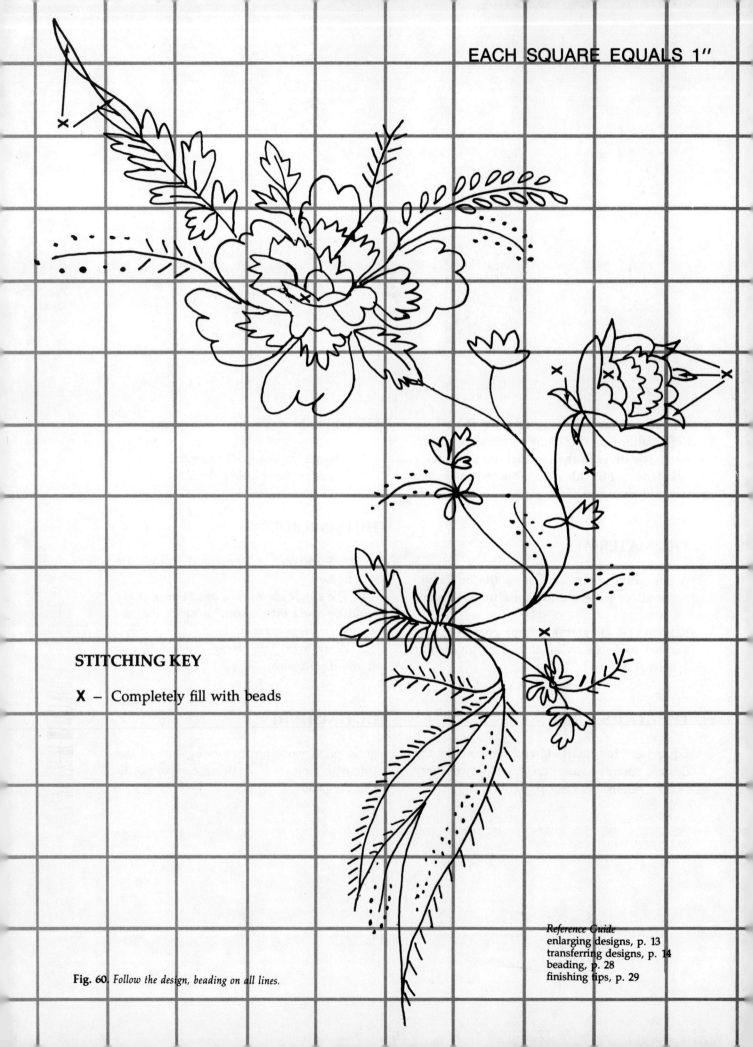

STITCHING KEY

X – Completely fill with beads

Fig. 60. *Follow the design, beading on all lines.*

Reference Guide
enlarging designs, p. 13
transferring designs, p. 14
beading, p. 28
finishing tips, p. 29

White silk shirt with white embroidery

Shown in color on page 36.

This classic white shirt with white embroidery is a fashionable addition to any wardrobe. The shirt shown here is made of white silk; other suitable fabrics are lightweight cottons, linen or wool.

THE MATERIALS

A classic white silk shirt similar to the one illustrated (or pattern and fabric to make your own)

8 spools white silk buttonhole twist

THE TOOLS

Equipment for enlarging and transferring the design, crewel or embroidery needle, small scissors, embroidery hoop

THE DESIGN

Note: The design is given for the right side of the shirt; it must be reversed (flopped) for the left side.

1. Enlarge the design (See Figure 61).
2. Transfer the enlarged design to the fabric.

THE EMBROIDERY

Put the work on the hoop and follow the stitching key.

1. Work all satin stitch areas first.
2. Work all flower centers next.
3. Work all stem stitch areas last.

THE FINISHING

Lightly press work on the wrong side of the fabric with a steam iron.

EACH SQUARE EQUALS 1″

Fig. 61. *Follow the design and stitching key.*

STITCHING KEY

A – Stem Stitch
S – Satin Stitch

CENTER

CENTER

LEFT SIDE (REVERSE FOR RIGHT SIDE)

Reference Guide
enlarging designs, p. 13
transferring designs, p. 14
stem stitch, p. 18
satin stitch, p. 20
finishing tips, p. 29

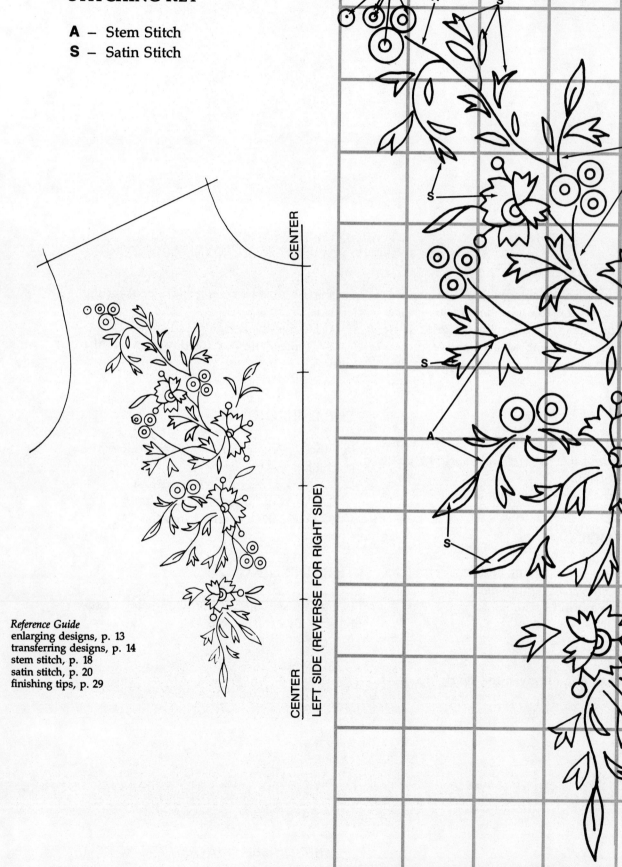

Placemats and napkins with scalloped edges

Shown in color on page 34.

THIS MODERN design is perfect for luncheons or informal dinners. For best results use linen fabric.

THE MATERIALS

2 maroon placemats, each approximately 13 by 16 inches (33 by 40 cm) (or linen fabric to make your own)

2 maroon napkins, each approximately 12 inches (30 cm) square (or linen fabric to make your own)

6 balls DMC #5 pearl cotton, 3 balls each in the following colors: emerald green #911 and yellow #742

Note: If you are making your own, 1 yard (1 m) of fabric will be enough.

THE TOOLS

Equipment for enlarging and transferring design, crewel or embroidery needle, small scissors, embroidery hoop

THE DESIGN

Note: The design is given for half of the placemat and one-quarter of the napkin. Reverse (flop) the design for the remainder of each placemat. The design on the napkin is just done on one corner, but the scalloped edges are continued all around.

1. Enlarge the designs (See Figure 62).

2. Transfer the enlarged design to the placemats.

3. Transfer the enlarged design to the napkins, placing it as shown. Include the scalloped edge all the way around the edge of the napkins.

THE EMBROIDERY

Put the work on the hoop and follow the stitching key.

1. Work the flowers first in satin stitch. Start by embroidering the centers and then fill the outside of flowers last.

2. Next, work all leaves and stems. The insides of the leaves are embroidered first with satin stitches and then the outlines of leaves and stems are done in stem stitches.

3. Work scallops in close buttonhole stitch.

THE FINISHING

1. Lightly press work on the wrong side of the fabric with a steam iron.

2. Trim away extra fabric around scallops with small scissors.

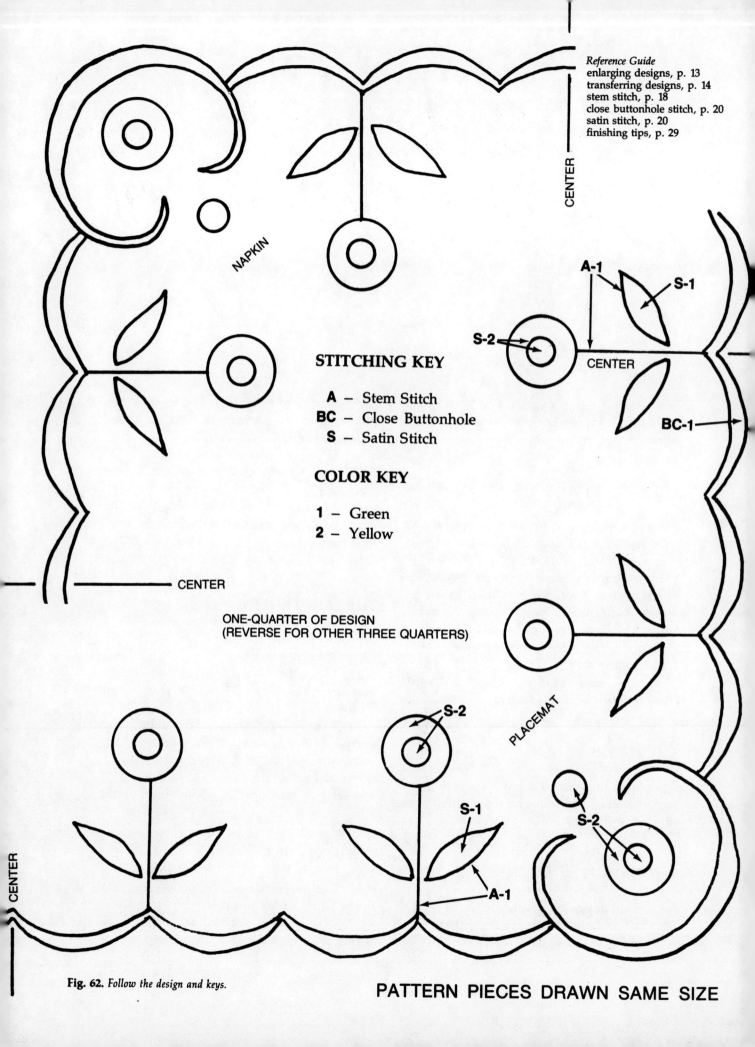

Reference Guide
enlarging designs, p. 13
transferring designs, p. 14
stem stitch, p. 18
close buttonhole stitch, p. 20
satin stitch, p. 20
finishing tips, p. 29

CENTER

NAPKIN

A-1

S-1

S-2

CENTER

BC-1

STITCHING KEY

A – Stem Stitch
BC – Close Buttonhole
S – Satin Stitch

COLOR KEY

1 – Green
2 – Yellow

CENTER

ONE-QUARTER OF DESIGN
(REVERSE FOR OTHER THREE QUARTERS)

PLACEMAT

S-2

S-1

S-2

A-1

CENTER

Fig. 62. *Follow the design and keys.*

PATTERN PIECES DRAWN SAME SIZE

Jacket with tone-on-tone embroidery

Shown in color on page 36.

This jacket, which features "tone-on-tone" embroidery, goes over a simple dress to make a smart costume. The design is suitable for wool, linen or piqué. Sheer or lightweight fabrics are not suitable.

Note: If you are making your own jacket, join front and back pieces as directed on the pattern instruction sheet. Do not attach sleeves or lining until embroidery is finished.

THE MATERIALS

A dress with a collarless jacket similar to the one illustrated (or pattern and fabric to make your own)
5 balls DMC #5 pearl cotton in a color to match fabric

THE TOOLS

Equipment for enlarging and transferring designs, crewel or embroidery needle, small scissors, embroidery hoop

THE DESIGN

1. Enlarge the design (See Figure 63).
2. Transfer the design to the fabric.

THE EMBROIDERY

Put the work on the hoop and follow the stitching key.
1. Work all the stems first.
2. Do the flowers and leaves next.
3. Work all the centers of flowers and leaves last.

THE FINISHING

Note: If you are making your own jacket, finish it now.

Lightly press work on the wrong side of the fabric with a steam iron.

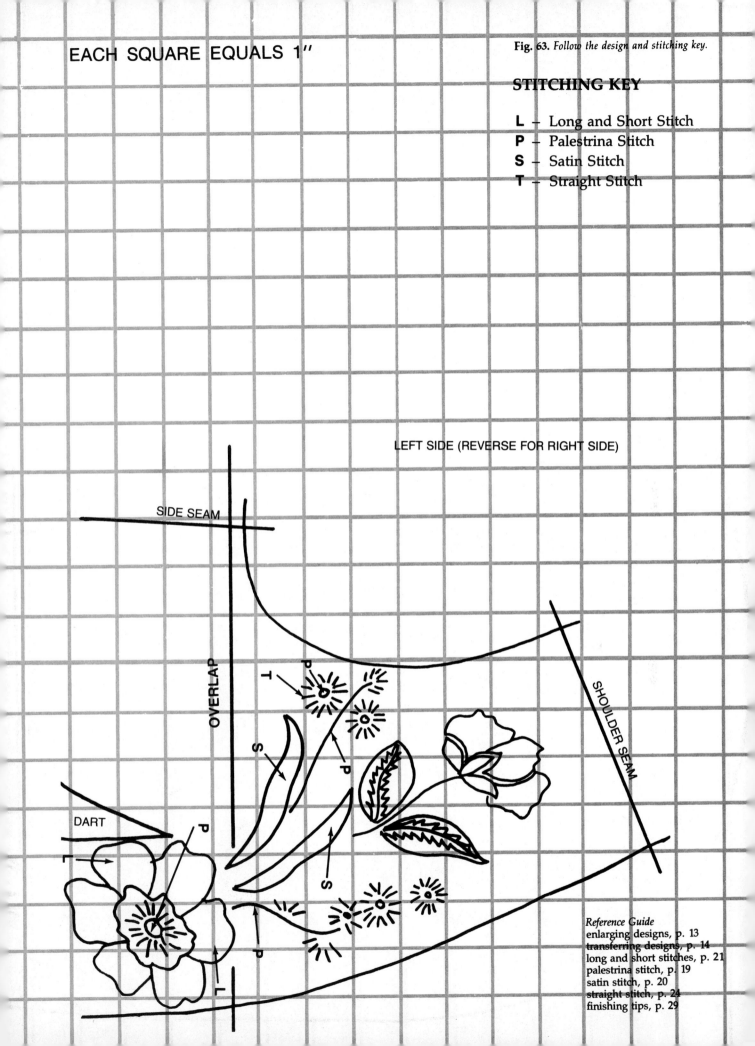

EACH SQUARE EQUALS 1"

Fig. 63. *Follow the design and stitching key.*

STITCHING KEY

L – Long and Short Stitch
P – Palestrina Stitch
S – Satin Stitch
T – Straight Stitch

LEFT SIDE (REVERSE FOR RIGHT SIDE)

SIDE SEAM

OVERLAP

SHOULDER SEAM

DART

Velvet embroidered pants

Shown in color on page 34.

THIS IS a Mexican-inspired design. It can also be done on corduroy, cotton or wool.

THE MATERIALS

A pair of velvet pants similar to the ones illustrated (or pattern and fabric to make your own)
1 skein golden yellow nylon twist

THE TOOLS

Equipment for enlarging and transferring the design, crewel or embroidery needle, small scissors

THE DESIGN

1. Enlarge the design (See Figure 64).

2. Transfer the enlarged design to the fabric, using the method for transferring onto pile fabrics.

THE EMBROIDERY

Follow the stitching key.
1. Work all stem stitch areas first.
2. Then work all lazy daisy stitch areas.
3. Next, work all straight stitch areas.
4. Work all seeding stitch areas last.

THE FINISHING

Lightly press work on the wrong side of the fabric with a steam iron.

Fig. 64. *Follow the design and stitching key.*

STITCHING KEY

A – Stem Stitch
D – Lazy Daisy
I – Seeding Stitch
T – Straight Stitch

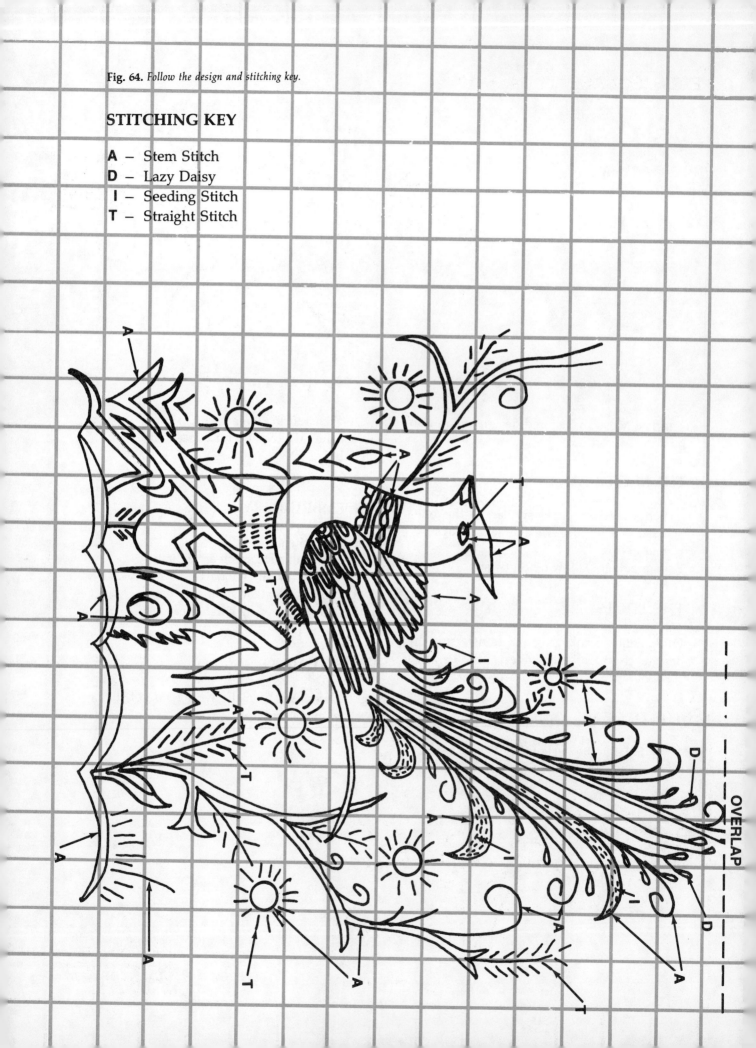

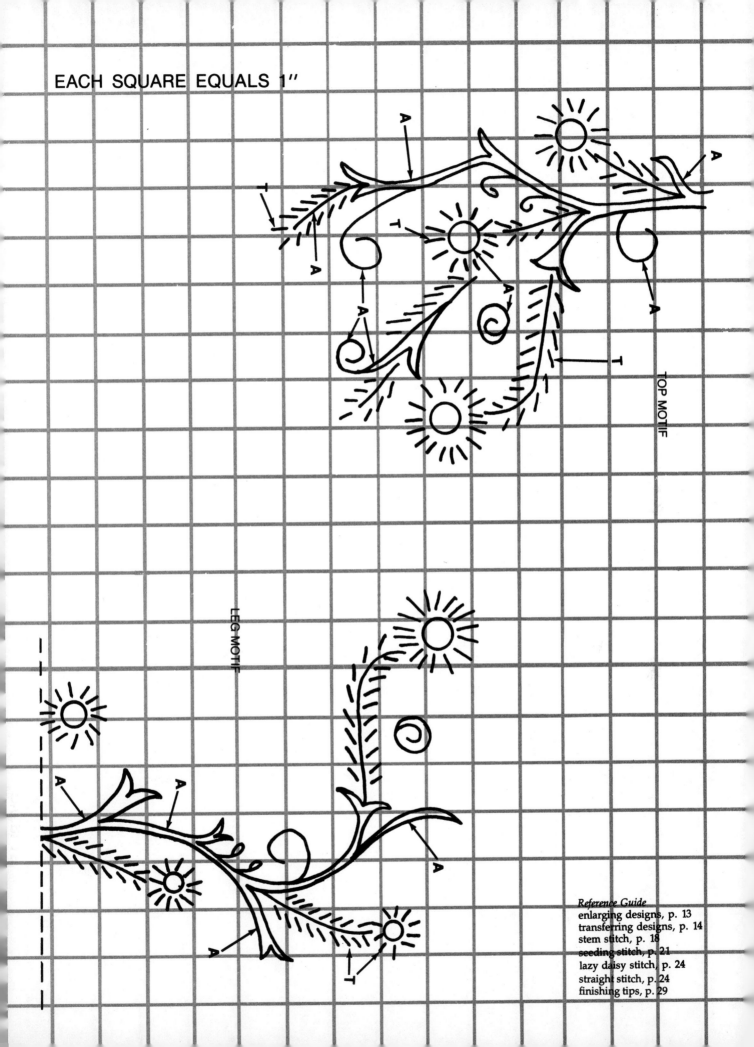

EACH SQUARE EQUALS 1"

TOP MOTIF

LEG MOTIF

Reference Guide
enlarging designs, p. 13
transferring designs, p. 14
stem stitch, p. 18
seeding stitch, p. 21
lazy daisy stitch, p. 24
straight stitch, p. 24
finishing tips, p. 29

Beige tablecloth with wrought-iron design

Shown in color on page 33.

THE DESIGN OF this lovely tablecloth imitates wrought iron. It is suitable for linen and cotton fabrics.

Note: If you are making your own tablecloth, cut it, baste a ½-inch (1.3-cm) hemline all around and mark the center.

THE MATERIALS

A ready-made tablecloth 52 inches (130 cm) square or the size required for your table (or 1¾ yards [1.75 m] beige linen to make your own)

12 skeins of DMC #5 pearl cotton in variegated orange #51

THE TOOLS

Equipment for enlarging and transferring the design, crewel or embroidery needle, small scissors, embroidery hoop

THE PREPARATION

If you are making your own tablecloth, turn in a hem ¼ inch (6 mm), baste and press. Turn in another hem 1 inch (2.5 cm). Baste, mitering corners, and press. If you are working with a ready-made tablecloth, rip out the hem and redo it in this manner.

THE DESIGN

Note: The center motif, side motif and corner motif are shown in Figure 65. The side and corner motifs are done four times.

1. Enlarge the designs (See Figure 65).
2. Transfer the enlarged designs to fabric. Run a line of stitches down the center of the cloth and line up the center of the design with the center of the fabric. The side motifs are placed 5 inches (12.5 cm) from the edges.

THE EMBROIDERY

Put the work on the hoop and follow the stitching key.

1. Work all center petals in satin stitch. Use threads of equal lengths for each petal to get uniform shaded effect.
2. Next, work all the large petals surrounding the satin stitch petals in Roman stitch.
3. Work all stem stitch areas.
4. Fill in the center of the large hearts with square filling stitch. For the type of square filling shown here, make the lengthwise lines one long stitch. Make the cross lines long stem stitches, catching two threads of the fabric at the intersections of the lengthwise thread. (See Figure 66.)
5. Work all French knots next.
6. Work all cross-stitches last.

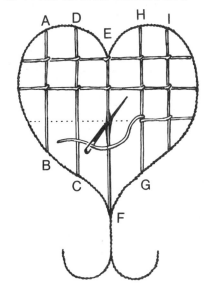

Fig. 66. *Special method of square filling.*

THE FINISHING

1. Finish hem with blindstitches and remove all basting stitches. Press.
2. Remove running stitches.
3. Lightly press entire tablecloth on the wrong side with a steam iron.

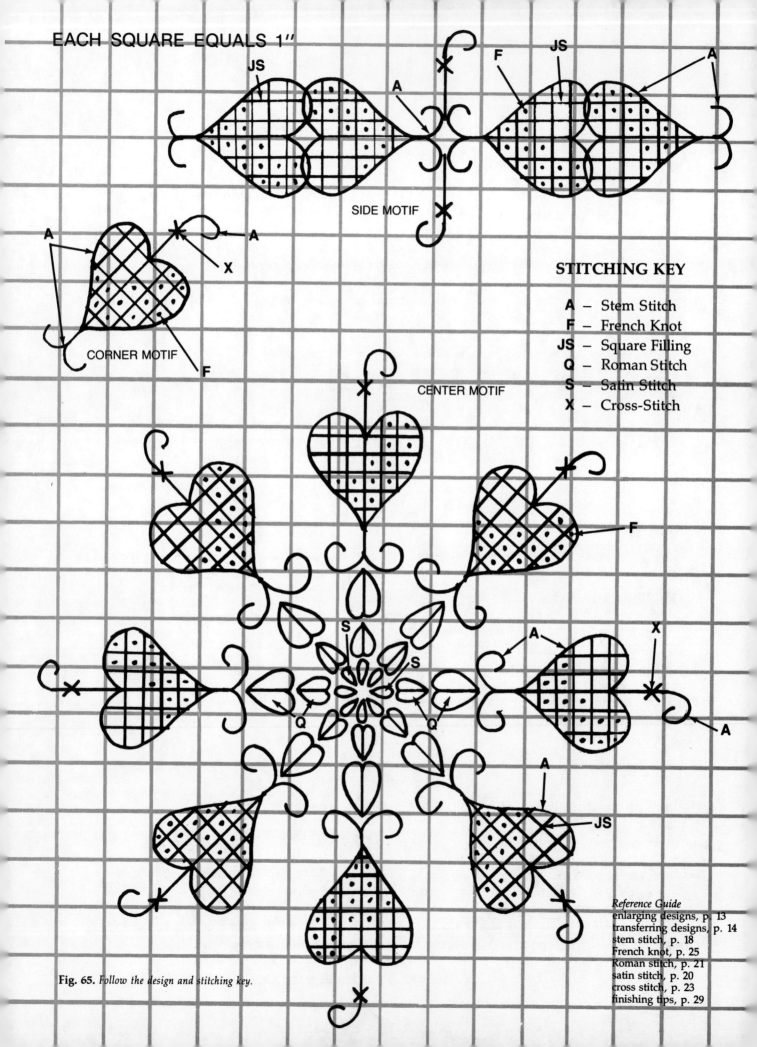

EACH SQUARE EQUALS 1"

SIDE MOTIF

CORNER MOTIF

CENTER MOTIF

STITCHING KEY

A – Stem Stitch
F – French Knot
JS – Square Filling
Q – Roman Stitch
S – Satin Stitch
X – Cross-Stitch

Fig. 65. *Follow the design and stitching key.*

Wild roses long evening dress

Shown in color on page 33.

A TRADITIONAL DESIGN worked with large-size stitches makes a quick-and-easy project. The design is suitable for medium-to-heavyweight fabrics, such as wool, wool worsted (like the one shown here), heavy linen or piqué.

Note: If you are making your own dress, you can transfer the design to the fabric before or after putting the dress together.

THE MATERIALS

A white dress similar to the one illustrated (or pattern and fabric to make your own)

13 balls DMC #5 pearl cotton in the following colors and quantities: 1 ball dark brown #801, 1 ball light brown #780, 2 balls red #816, 1 ball red #309, 2 balls emerald green #912, 2 balls dark green #909, 1 ball pink #899, 1 ball pink #716, 1 ball yellow #743 and 1 ball black #310

THE TOOLS

Equipment for enlarging and transferring the design, crewel or embroidery needle, small scissors, embroidery hoop

THE DESIGN

1. Enlarge the design (See Figure 67).
2. Transfer the enlarged design to the fabric.

THE EMBROIDERY

Put the work on the hoop and follow the stitching key.

1. Work all satin stitch areas first.
2. Next, work all long and short stitch areas.
3. Then work all stem stitch areas.
4. Work all straight stitches and French knots last.

THE FINISHING

Note: If you are making your own dress, finish according to pattern directions. Press again.

Lightly press work on the wrong side of the fabric with a steam iron.

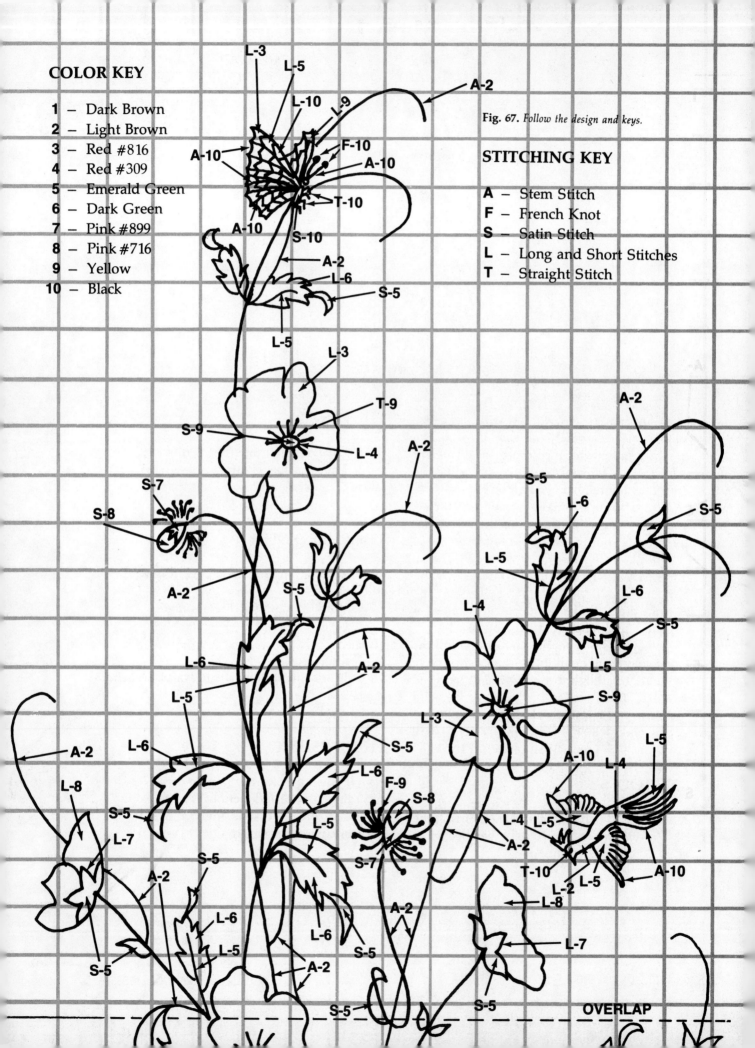

COLOR KEY

1 – Dark Brown
2 – Light Brown
3 – Red #816
4 – Red #309
5 – Emerald Green
6 – Dark Green
7 – Pink #899
8 – Pink #716
9 – Yellow
10 – Black

Fig. 67. *Follow the design and keys.*

STITCHING KEY

A – Stem Stitch
F – French Knot
S – Satin Stitch
L – Long and Short Stitches
T – Straight Stitch

OVERLAP

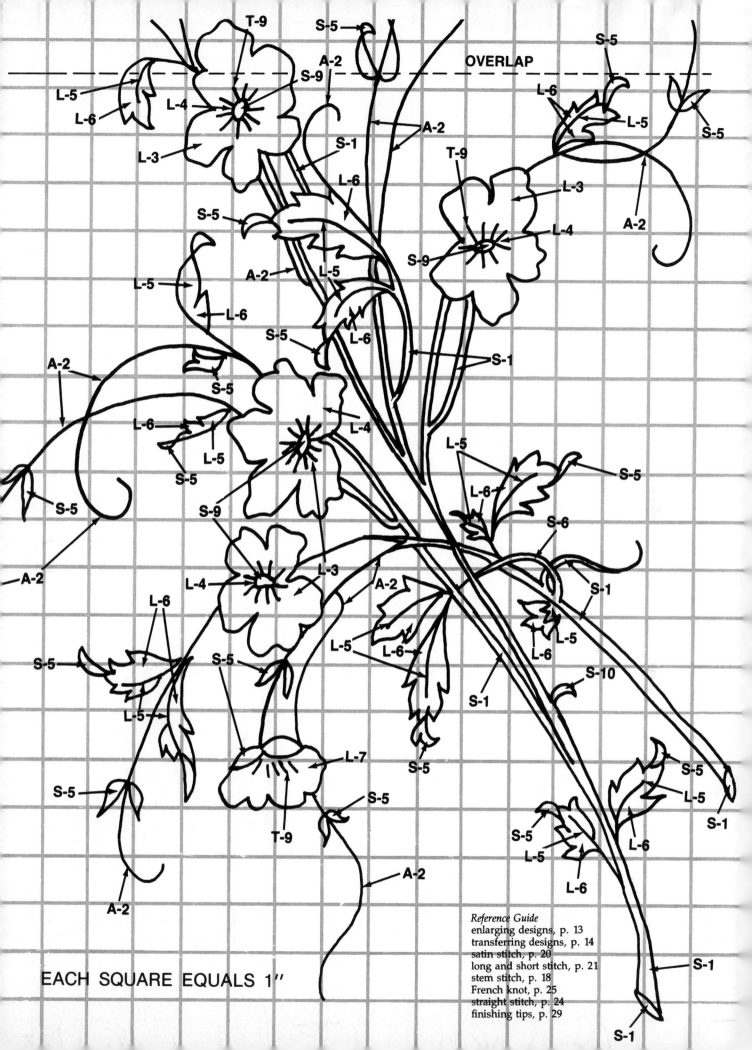

Breakfast set with Portuguese embroidery

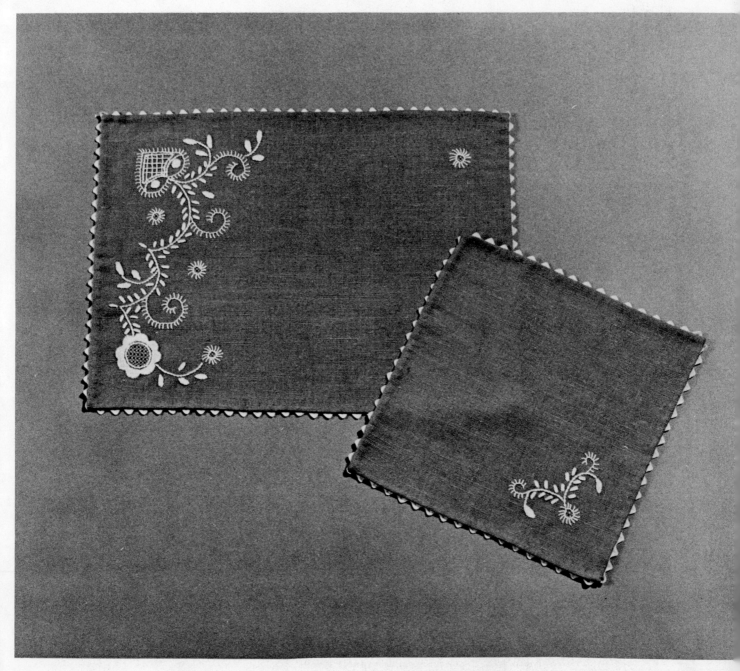

Shown in color on page 35.

This charming breakfast set consists of a tray cloth and napkins. Bright red linen was selected as the best background for the quick-and-easy Portuguese embroidery done in white. The design is also suitable for cotton fabrics.

THE MATERIALS

A red linen tray cloth large enough to fit your tray (or fabric to make your own)
2 napkins (or fabric to make your own)
6 balls white DMC #5 pearl cotton
3 yards white medium rickrack trim for edges

THE TOOLS

Equipment for enlarging and transferring the design, crewel or embroidery needle, tapestry needle, small scissors, embroidery hoop

THE DESIGN

1. Enlarge the designs (See Figure 68).
2. Transfer the enlarged design to the tray

cover, placing it 2½ inches (6.5 cm) from the edge.
3. Transfer the enlarged design to the napkin.

THE EMBROIDERY

Put the work on the hoop and follow the stitching key. Embroider the design in any order you like, but the square filling must be finished last.

Small leaves (except those marked for satin stitch) in the design are done by making three straight stitches as close together as possible. Make the center stitch first. The two outer stitches are made by inserting the thread one thread away from the center stitch.

THE FINISHING

1. Sew rickrack trim on all pieces around edges.
2. Lightly press all pieces on the wrong side of the fabric with a steam iron.

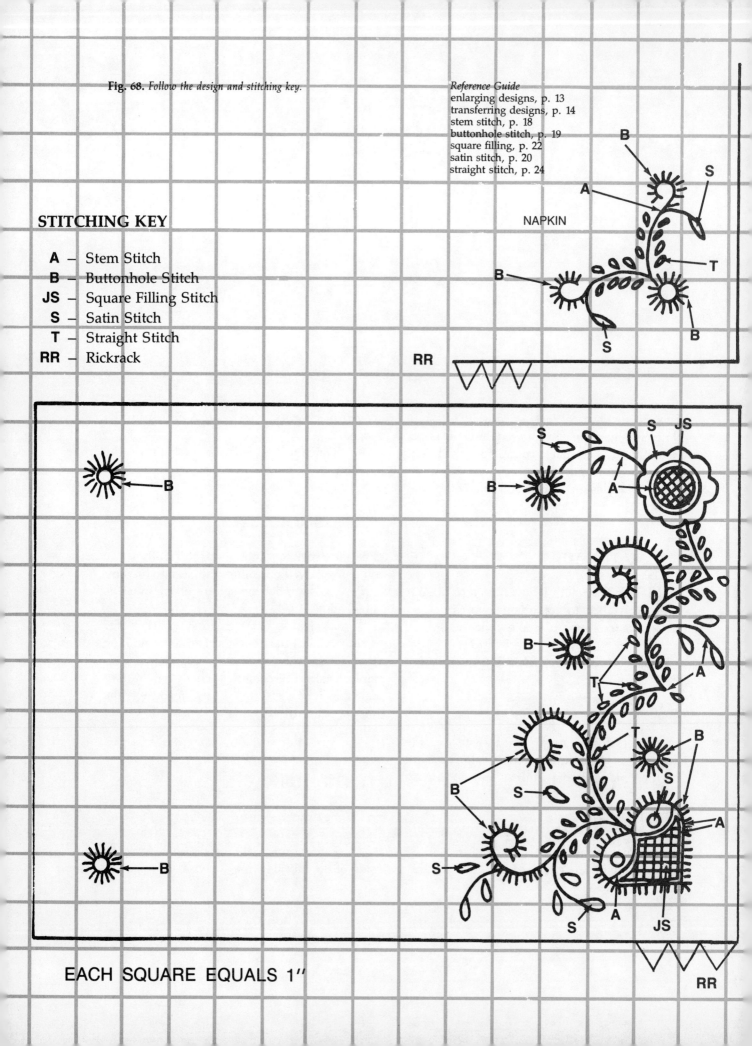

Fig. 68. *Follow the design and stitching key.*

Reference Guide
enlarging designs, p. 13
transferring designs, p. 14
stem stitch, p. 18
buttonhole stitch, p. 19
square filling, p. 22
satin stitch, p. 20
straight stitch, p. 24

NAPKIN

STITCHING KEY

A – Stem Stitch
B – Buttonhole Stitch
JS – Square Filling Stitch
S – Satin Stitch
T – Straight Stitch
RR – Rickrack

EACH SQUARE EQUALS 1"

Floral pattern luncheon set

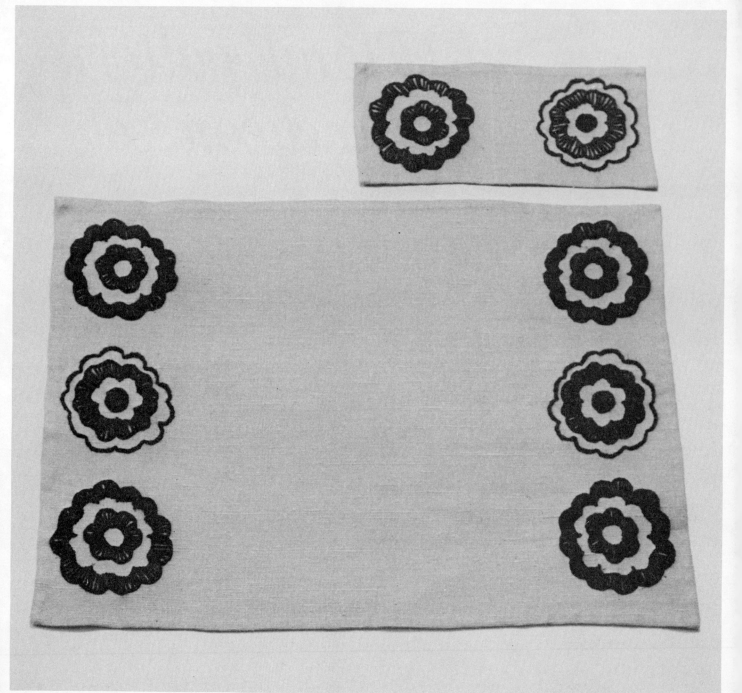

Shown in color on page 33.

THE FLOWER DESIGN shown here is simple and easy to make. It is made on linen fabric, but can be done just as well on cotton.

THE MATERIALS

¾ yard (0.70 m) shocking pink linen (enough for 2 placemats and 2 coasters)
7 skeins DMC Article #89 mat-finish cotton embroidery twist in navy #2826

THE TOOLS

Equipment for enlarging and transferring the design, crewel or embroidery needle, small scissors, embroidery hoop

THE PREPARATION

1. For placemats measure and cut two rectangles 13½ by 18½ inches (34.3 by 46.5 cm). For coasters measure and cut two rectangles 4½ by 8½ inches (11.5 by 21.5 cm).

2. Hem each piece before embroidering. Turn up a hem ¼ inch (6 mm) wide, baste and press. Turn up another ¼-inch (6-mm) hem, baste and press. Finish hems with hemstitch (seamstress' hemstitch, not embroiderer's hemstitch). Remove basting stitches.

THE DESIGN

1. Enlarge the design (See Figure 69).
2. Transfer the enlarged design to the fabric, placing it ¾ inch (2 cm) from the hem.

THE EMBROIDERY

Put the work on the hoop and follow the stitching key. Do stitches in any order you like.

THE FINISHING

Lightly press all pieces on the wrong side with a steam iron.

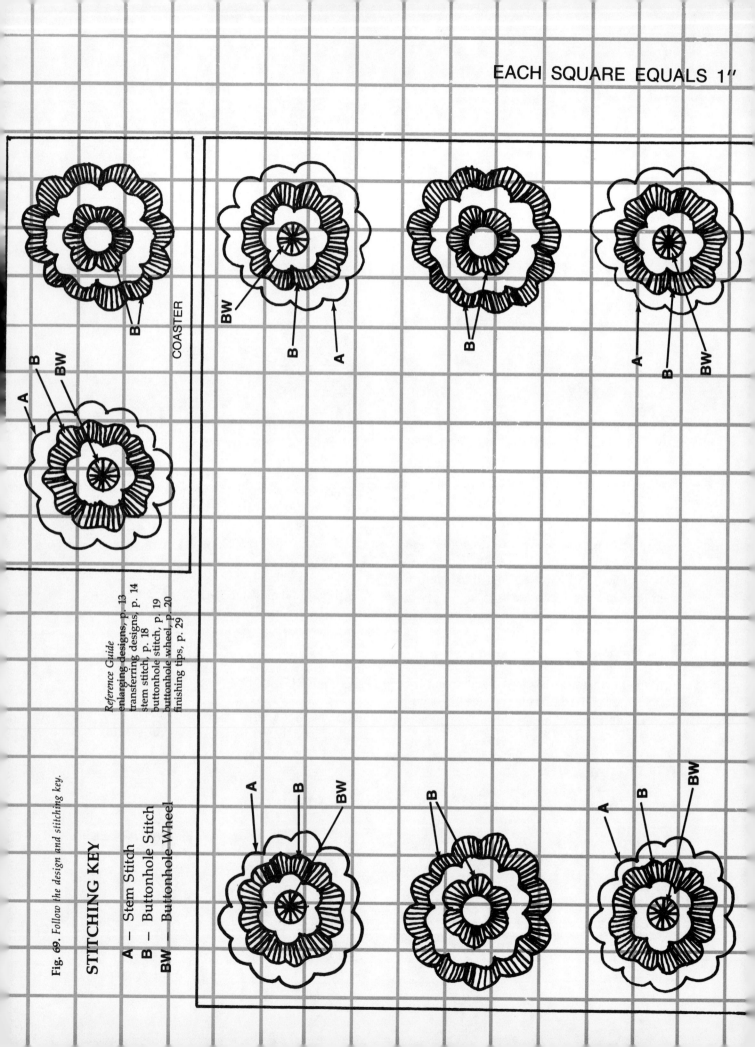

Fig. 69. Follow the design and stitching key.

STITCHING KEY

A — Stem Stitch
B — Buttonhole Stitch
BW — Buttonhole Wheel

Reference Guide
enlarging designs, p. 13
transferring designs, p. 14
stem stitch, p. 18
buttonhole stitch, p. 19
buttonhole wheel, p. 20
finishing tips, p. 29

COASTER

A
B
BW
B

BW
B
A

B

A
B
BW

A
B
BW

B

A
B
BW

Embroidered lemonade set

Shown in color on page 36.

This is a design that works well on linen or cotton fabric. The materials given here are enough for one tray cloth and eight coasters.

THE MATERIALS

½ yard (0.50 m) yellow linen
6 balls DMC #5 pearl cotton in celery green

THE TOOLS

Equipment for enlarging the design, crewel or embroidery needle, small scissors, embroidery hoop

THE DESIGN

1. Enlarge the design (See Figure 70).

2. Transfer the enlarged design to the fabric.

THE EMBROIDERY

Put the work on the hoop and follow the stitching key.
1. Work all stem stitch areas first.
2. Next, work all satin stitch areas.
3. Work all close buttonhole stitch areas last.

THE FINISHING

1. Lightly press all pieces on the wrong side of the fabric with a steam iron.
2. Trim off excess fabric, taking care not to cut the embroidery thread. Press again if necessary.

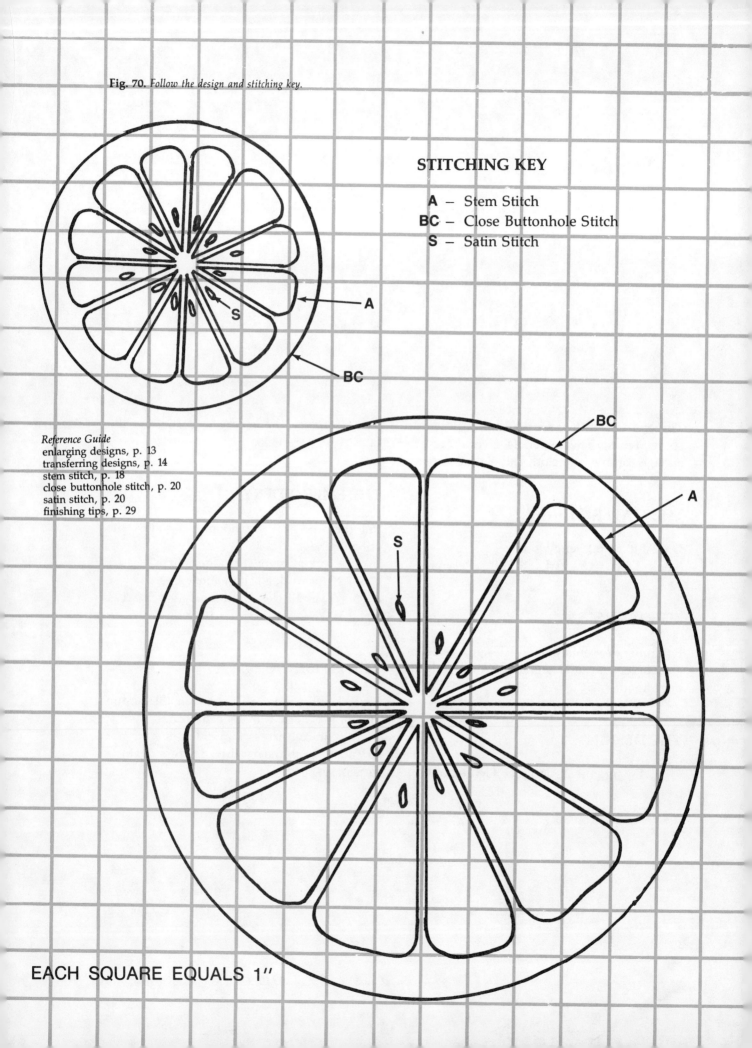

Fig. 70. *Follow the design and stitching key.*

STITCHING KEY

A – Stem Stitch
BC – Close Buttonhole Stitch
S – Satin Stitch

Reference Guide
enlarging designs, p. 13
transferring designs, p. 14
stem stitch, p. 18
close buttonhole stitch, p. 20
satin stitch, p. 20
finishing tips, p. 29

EACH SQUARE EQUALS 1″

Quick wraparound robe

Shown in color on page 36.

This wraparound robe can be made from scratch in a jiffy. The robe shown here is made of stretch terry, but the design is suitable for cotton or heavy linen fabrics.

THE MATERIALS

1½ yards (1.40 m) stretch terry cloth (more or less depending on height)
½ yard (0.50 m) lining fabric
9 skeins DMC #3 pearl cotton, 1 skein each in the following colors: green #909, green #911, green #319, brown #790, orange #947, gray #414, blue #797, white, and black
2 balls DMC #5 pearl cotton, 1 ball each in the following colors: red #321, yellow #444
1 package Velcro® fasteners
1 piece of elastic for casing at the top

THE TOOLS

Equipment for enlarging and transferring the design, crewel or embroidery needle, small scissors, embroidery hoop

THE DESIGN

Note: The design is placed on back of the robe. Mark the center back of the robe and match it up with the center of the design.

1. Enlarge the design (Figure 71).
2. Transfer the enlarged design to the fabric, placing it beginning 2 inches (5 cm) from the edge and following directions for transferring onto terry cloth (Figure 72).

THE EMBROIDERY

1. Line the area to be embroidered.
2. Put work on the hoop and follow the stitching key.
3. Proceed to embroider design in any order you like.

THE FINISHING

1. Lightly press embroidery on the wrong side with a steam iron.
2. To finish robe, turn in a 1-inch (2.5-cm) hem for casing across the top edge and machine stitch. Insert the elastic. Sew Velcro® fasteners 2 inches (5 cm) and 3 inches (7.5 cm) from the two edges. Turn in a 1-inch (2.5-cm) hem at each side and machine stitch. Turn in a 2-inch (5-cm) hem at lower edge and machine stitch. Press.

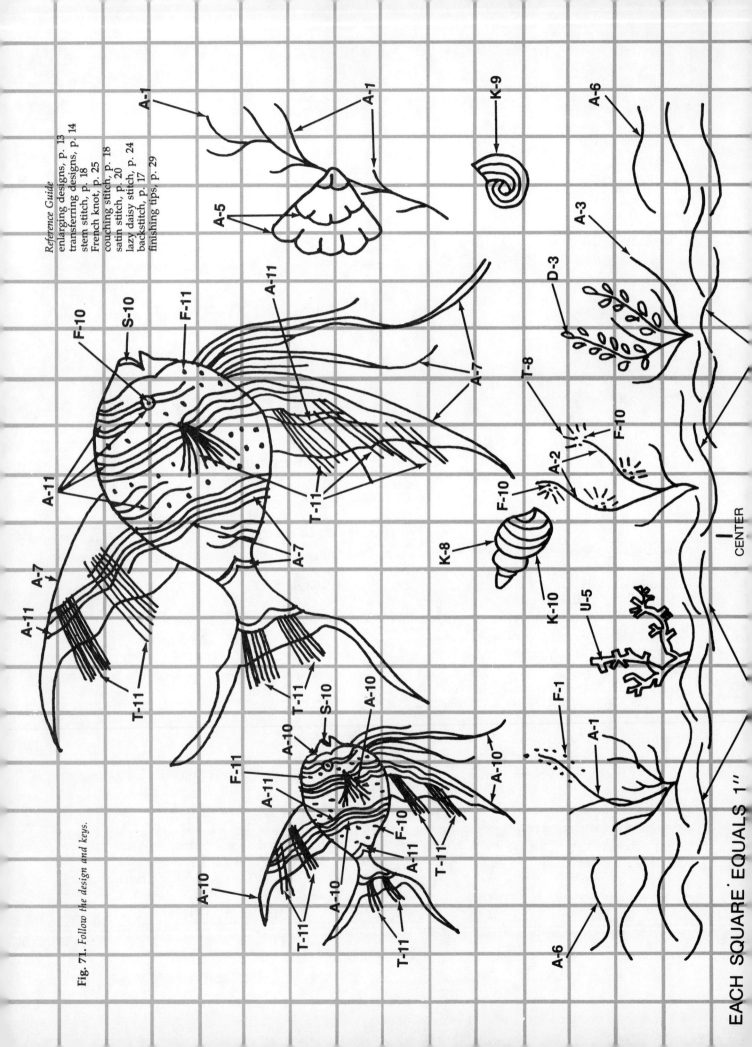

Fig. 71. Follow the design and keys.

Reference Guide
enlarging designs, p. 13
transferring designs, p. 14
stem stitch, p. 18
French knot, p. 25
couching stitch, p. 18
satin stitch, p. 20
lazy daisy stitch, p. 24
backstitch, p. 17
finishing tips, p. 29

EACH SQUARE EQUALS 1"

STITCHING KEY

A – Stem Stitch
F – French Knot
K – Couching
S – Satin Stitch
D – Lazy Daisy
U – Backstitch

COLOR KEY

1 – Green #909
2 – Green #911
3 – Green #319
4 – Brown
5 – Orange
6 – Gray
7 – Blue
8 – White
9 – Black
10 – Red
11 – Yellow

Fig. 72. *Positioning the design.*

Back

Card tablecloth for bridge

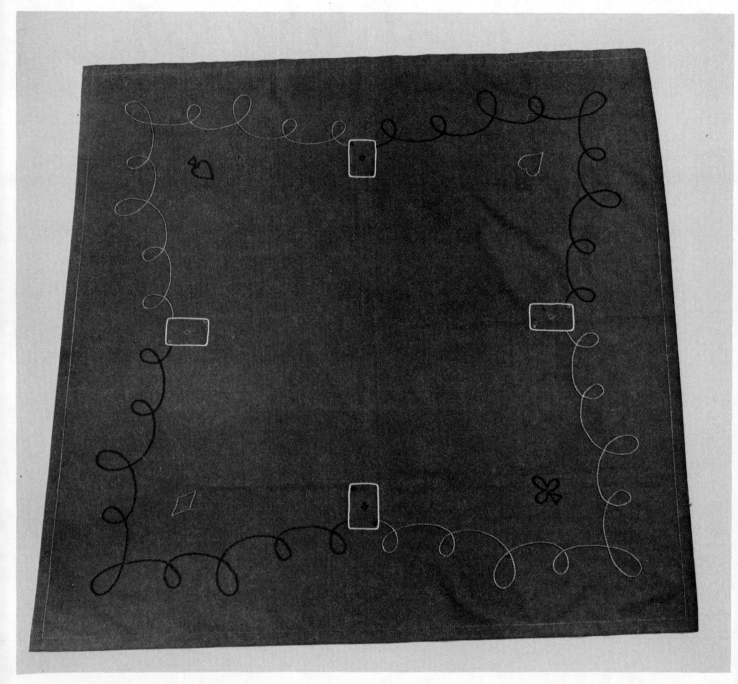

Shown in color on page 35.

THE PLAYING CARD MOTIF makes this tablecloth a fun project. It is small enough for you to do quickly, so it doesn't require a large investment of time. The design is suitable for cotton, linen, wool or felt.

Note: If you are making your own tablecloth, hem the piece by turning ¼ inch (6 mm) in; baste and press. Then turn in 1 inch (2.5 cm), baste and press.

THE MATERIALS

- A 52-inch (130-cm) square green tablecloth (or 1½ yard [1.5 m] green cotton to make your own)
- 3 balls DMC #5 pearl cotton, 1 ball each in the following colors: red, black and white
- 1 skein 6-strand embroidery floss to match fabric

THE TOOLS

Equipment for enlarging and transferring the design, crewel or embroidery needle, small scissors, embroidery hoop

THE DESIGN

Note: The design shown represents one-quarter of the total design. Reverse ("flop") the design for the other three-quarters, substituting the appropriate playing card and symbol in their positions.

1. Enlarge the design (See Figure 73).
2. Transfer the enlarged design to the fabric, placing it as shown in Figure 74. Run a line of stitches down the center of your fabric to serve as a guide and match up with center of the design.

THE EMBROIDERY

Put the work on the hoop and follow the stitching key.

1. Work the outline (tendril-like lines) of the design first.
2. Work the playing cards last.
3. Using three strands of floss, work in line of stem stitches on the right side of the fabric, just where the top edge of the hem stops. Stitch hem on the wrong side with hemstitch (seamstress's hemstitch, not embroiderer's). The hemstitches should catch the back threads of the stem stitches and not the fabric.

THE FINISHING

1. Remove running stitches and basting.
2. Lightly press work on the wrong side of fabric with a steam iron.

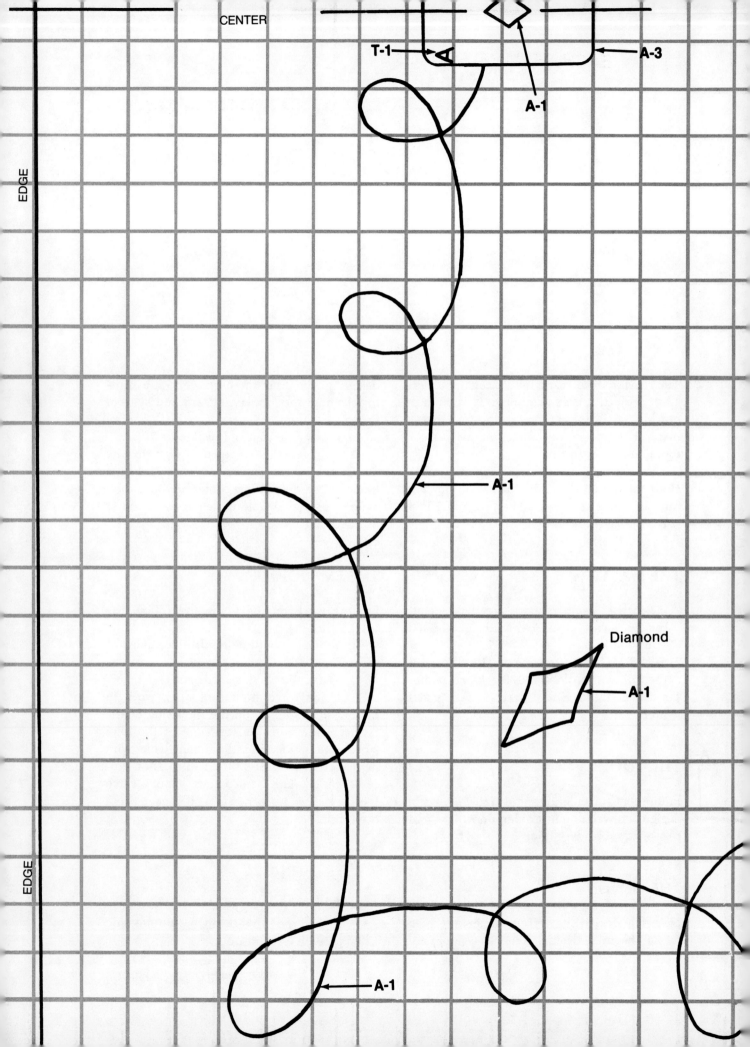

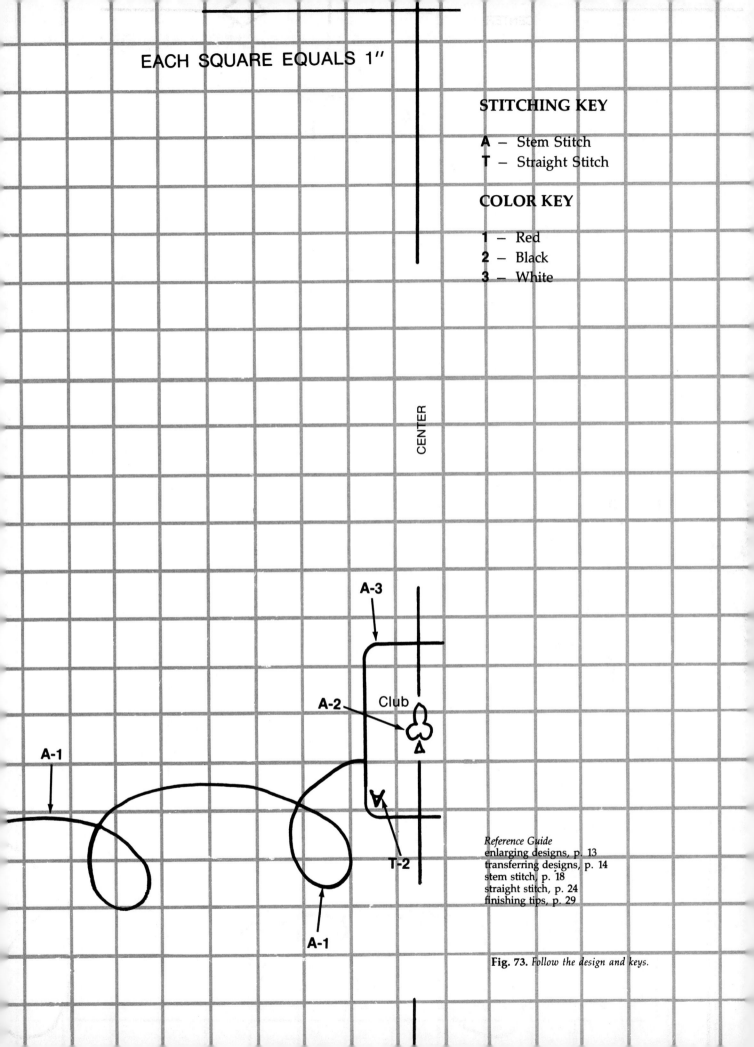

EACH SQUARE EQUALS 1"

STITCHING KEY

A – Stem Stitch
T – Straight Stitch

COLOR KEY

1 – Red
2 – Black
3 – White

CENTER

A-3

A-2

Club

A-1

T-2

A-1

Reference Guide
enlarging designs, p. 13
transferring designs, p. 14
stem stitch, p. 18
straight stitch, p. 24
finishing tips, p. 29

Fig. 73. *Follow the design and keys.*

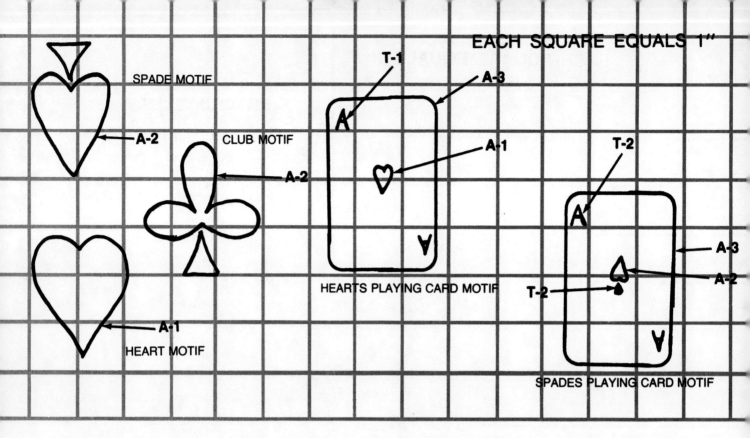

SPADE MOTIF

A-2

CLUB MOTIF

A-2

T-1

A-3

A-1

HEARTS PLAYING CARD MOTIF

T-2

A-3

A-2

T-2

SPADES PLAYING CARD MOTIF

A-1

HEART MOTIF

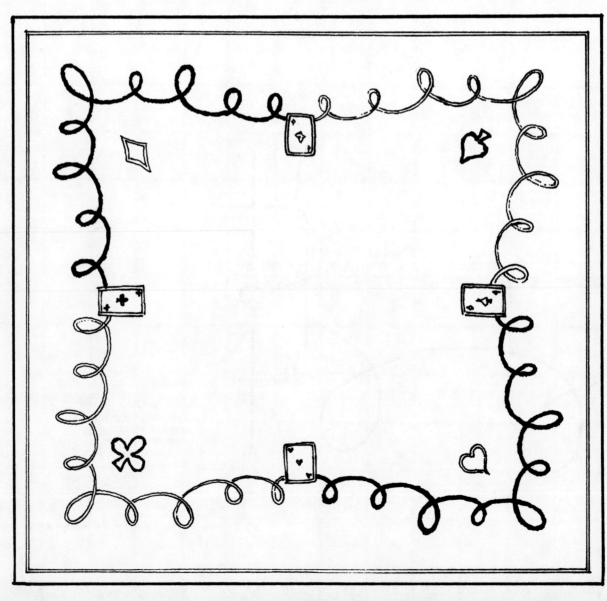

Table runner with feather design

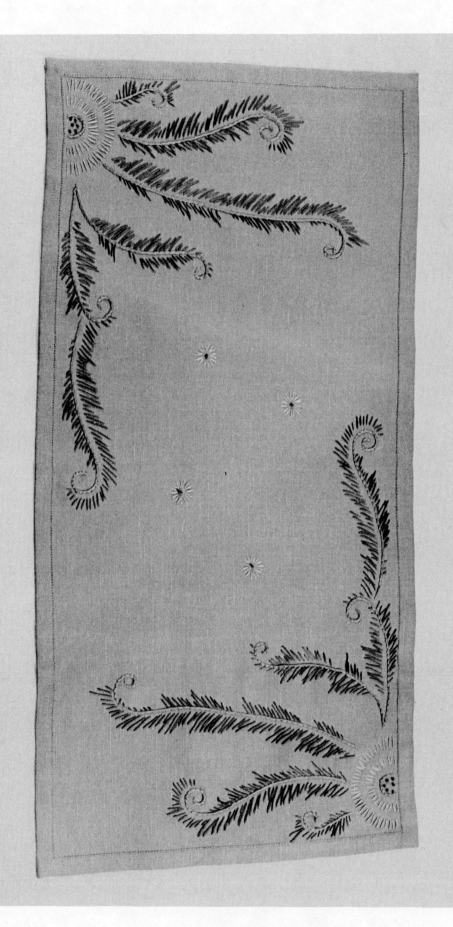

Shown in color on page 34.

Two SIMPLE STITCHES are combined to make this a quick-and-easy project. This design is suitable for linen or cotton fabrics.

THE MATERIALS

½ yard (approximately 0.50 m) green linen or cotton

6 skeins DMC 6-strand embroidery floss in the following amounts and colors: 3 skeins brown #919, 2 skeins brown #832 and 1 skein yellow #977

THE TOOLS

Equipment for enlarging and transferring the design, crewel or embroidery needle, small scissors, embroidery hoop

THE PREPARATION

1. Draw and cut a rectangle 35 by 18 inches (87.5 by 45 cm).

2. Hem the piece by turning in ¼ inch (6 mm), baste and press. Turn in 1 inch (2.5 cm), baste and press.

THE DESIGN

Note: The design shown represents half of the total design. Reverse ("flop") it for the other half, repeating just the flower on the left.

1. Enlarge the design (See Figure 75).

2. Transfer the enlarged design to the fabric, placing it 1 inch (2.5 cm) from the hem.

THE EMBROIDERY

Put the work on the hoop and follow the stitching key. Use six strands of floss throughout the work.

1. Work the bars that form the feathers first.

2. Continue with the rest of the work in any order you like.

3. Using three strands of floss, work a line of stem stitch on the right side of the fabric, just where the top edge of the hem stops (Figures 76 a and b). Stitch hem on the wrong side with hemstitch (seamstress's hemstitch, not embroiderer's). The hemstitches catch the back threads of the stem stitches and not the fabric.

THE FINISHING

1. Remove basting stitches.

2. Lightly press work on the wrong side of the fabric with a steam iron.

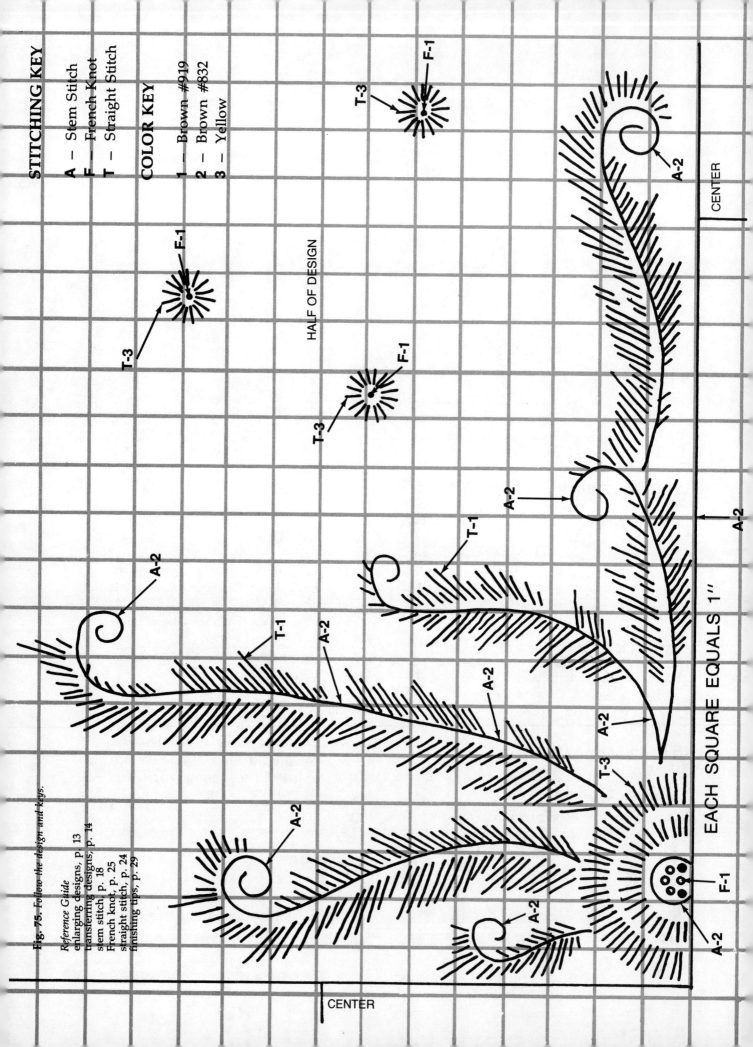

Fig. 75. *Follow the design and keys.*

Reference Guide
enlarging designs, p. 13
transferring designs, p. 14
stem stitch, p. 18
French knot, p. 25
straight stitch, p. 24
finishing tips, p. 29

STITCHING KEY

A – Stem Stitch
F – French Knot
T – Straight Stitch

COLOR KEY

1 – Brown #919
2 – Brown #832
3 – Yellow

HALF OF DESIGN

EACH SQUARE EQUALS 1″

CENTER

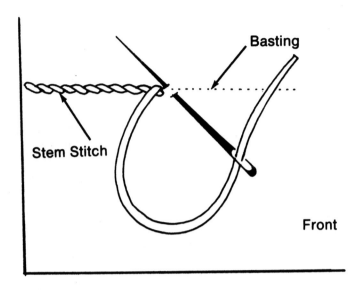

Fig. 76 a. *Stitching along the edge.*

Fig. 76 b.

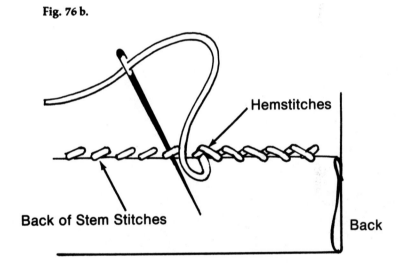

Skirt with embroidered border design

Shown in color on page 35.

This design is suitable for long or short skirts, and the suggested fabrics are lightweight wool, linen or cotton.

THE MATERIALS

An A-line skirt similar to the one illustrated
  (or fabric and pattern to make your own)
15 yards (13.75 m) white baby rickrack
basting thread
5 balls white DMC #5 pearl cotton
1 skein of 6-strand embroidery floss in white

THE TOOLS

Equipment for enlarging and transferring the design, embroidery or crewel needle, tapestry needle, small scissors, embroidery hoop

THE PREPARATION

Run a line of basting stitches to mark the hemline. Press hem open.

THE DESIGN

1. Enlarge the design (See Figure 77).

2. Transfer the enlarged design to the fabric, placing the lower edge of the design ¼ inch (6 mm) from the basted hemline.

THE EMBROIDERY

Put the work on the hoop and follow the stitching key.
1. Work all satin stitch areas first.
2. Work all buttonhole stitch areas next.
3. Cover all areas that call for square filling stitch.
4. Attach the rickrack using the overcast stitch with two strands of embroidery floss.

THE FINISHING

Note: If you are making your own skirt, finish as directed on the pattern.
1. Lightly press work on the wrong side of the fabric with a steam iron.
2. Turn up hem along the basted hemline and finish with hemstitch (seamstress's hemstitch). Press.

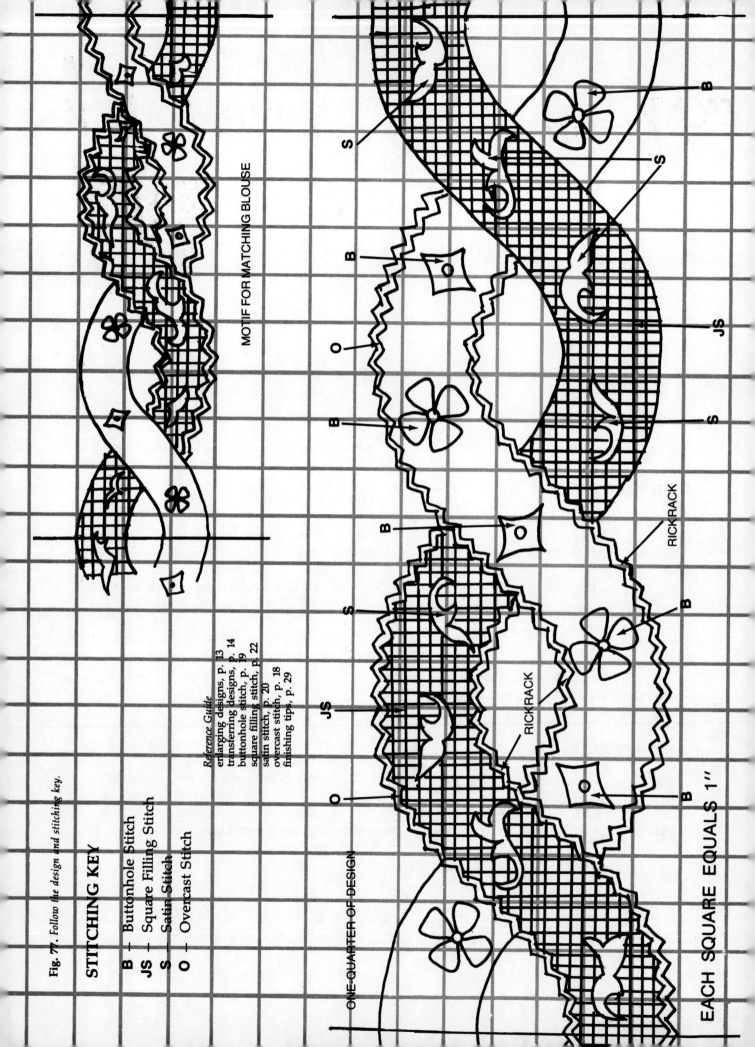

Fig. 77. Follow the design and stitching key.

STITCHING KEY

B – Buttonhole Stitch
JS – Square Filling Stitch
S – Satin Stitch
O – Overcast Stitch

Reference Guide
enlarging designs, p. 13
transferring designs, p. 14
buttonhole stitch, p. 19
square filling stitch, p. 22
satin stitch, p. 20
overcast stitch, p. 18
finishing tips, p. 29

MOTIF FOR MATCHING BLOUSE

RICKRACK

RICKRACK

ONE-QUARTER OF DESIGN

EACH SQUARE EQUALS 1"

"No Smoking" tablecloth and cushion

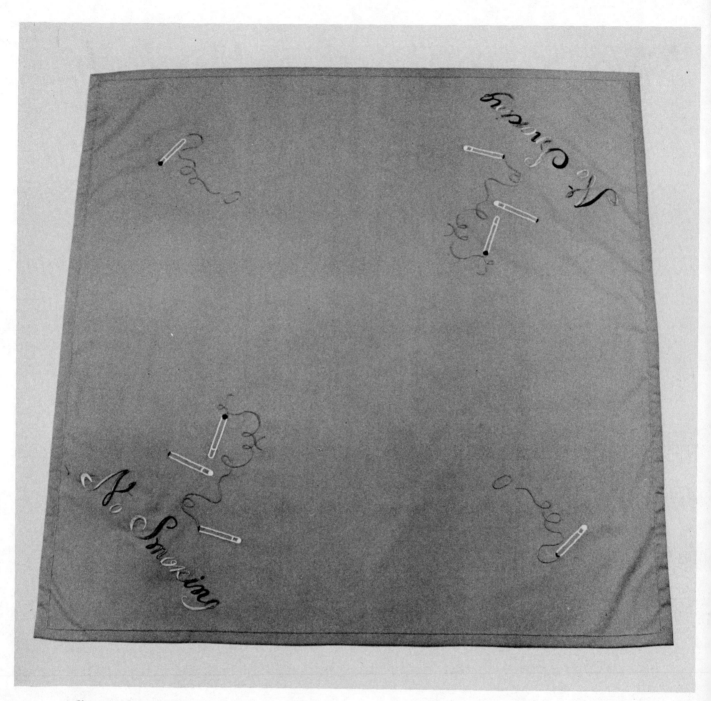

Shown in color on page 34.

The design of this tablecloth and matching pillow cover is also suitable for the front of a T-shirt. The tablecloth and pillow cover can be made of cotton linen, felt or sailcloth.

THE MATERIALS

2 yards (approximately 2 m) red cotton fabric for tablecloth (50 inches [125 cm] square) and pillow (18 inches [45 cm] square)
6 balls DMC #5 pearl cotton in each of the following colors and quantities: 1 ball gray #414, 1 ball black #310, 1 ball white, and 3 balls shaded black #53 (for letters)
1 skein 6-strand embroidery floss in color to match

THE TOOLS

Equipment for enlarging and transferring the design, crewel or embroidery needle, small scissors, embroidery hoop

THE PREPARATION

1. Cut the fabric for the tablecloth and pillow.
2. Hem the tablecloth fabric by turning in ¼ inch (6 mm), basting and then pressing. Then turn in 1 inch (2.5 cm), baste and press.

THE DESIGN

1. Enlarge the design (See Figure 78).
2. Transfer the enlarged design to the fabric as shown in Figures 79 and 80.

THE EMBROIDERY

Put the work on the hoop and follow the stitching key. The stem stitch is the only stitch used.

1. Work all the cigarettes first. Do the outlining first and then fill in as indicated.
2. Next, work the smoke scrolls.
3. Work the "No Smoking" lettering mostly with only the darkest parts of the shaded variegated thread.
Note: Save the lightest sections of the thread for another project.
4. Using three strands of floss, work a line of stem stitches on the right side of the fabric, just where the top edge of the hem stops. Stitch hem on the wrong side with hemstitch (seamstress's hemstitch, not embroiderer's). The hemstitches catch the back threads of the stem stitches and not the fabric.

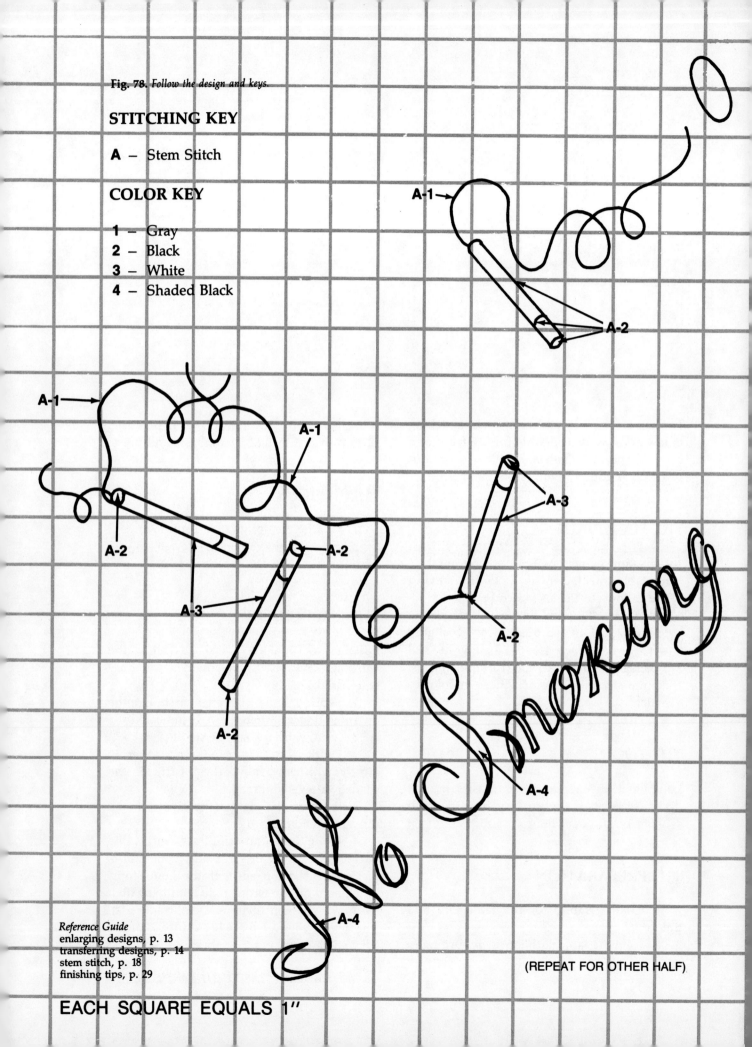

Fig. 78. *Follow the design and keys.*

STITCHING KEY

A – Stem Stitch

COLOR KEY

1 – Gray
2 – Black
3 – White
4 – Shaded Black

A-1

A-2

A-1

A-1

A-2

A-3

A-2

A-3

A-2

A-2

A-3

A-2

A-4

A-4

(REPEAT FOR OTHER HALF)

EACH SQUARE EQUALS 1″

THE FINISHING

1. Lightly press all work on the wrong side with a steam iron.

2. Stitch the two pillow pieces with right sides together on three sides. Turn inside out and slip in pillow form. Stitch the fourth side closed with slip stitches.

Note: Figure 81 shows the "No Smoking" design used on a T-shirt.

Fig. 81. *Positioning the design on a T-shirt.*

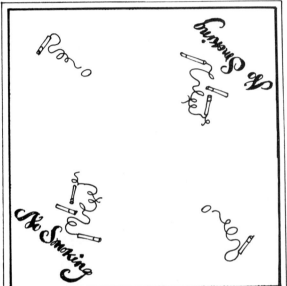

Fig. 79. *Positioning on tablecloth.*

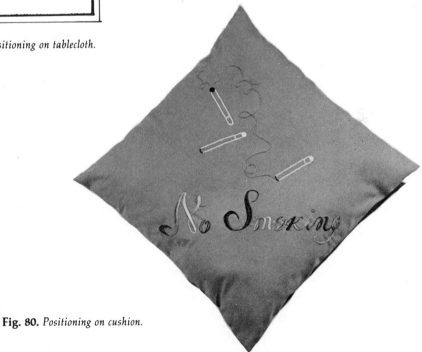

Fig. 80. *Positioning on cushion.*

Green leaves
evening dress

Shown in color on page 35.

ON THIS WHITE evening dress one green leaf is appliquéd and the other adjacent leaf is embroidered with green thread. The dress is suitable for linen, wool, piqué (as shown here in the photograph) or any medium-to-heavy-weight fabrics.

THE MATERIALS

A long white evening dress similar to the one illustrated (or pattern and fabric to make your own)

⅓ yard (30 cm) of green fabric

4 skeins DMC #3 pearl cotton in the following colors and quantities: 2 skeins green (to match fabric), 2 skeins white

THE TOOLS

Equipment for enlarging and transferring the design, crewel or embroidery needle, small scissors, embroidery hoop

THE DESIGN

1. Enlarge the design (See Figure 82).
2. Transfer the design to the dress fabric.
3. Transfer the leaf design to the green fabric and cut out the required number of leaves. Turn under the edges, pin and baste leaves in place on the dress. Alternate the appliquéd and embroidered flowers as indicated in the photograph.

THE EMBROIDERY

1. Work buttonhole stitch all around both the embroidered and the appliquéd leaves.
2. Work chain stitch in the center of both the appliquéd and the embroidered leaves.

THE FINISHING

1. Remove all basting.
2. Lightly press fabric on the wrong side with a steam iron.

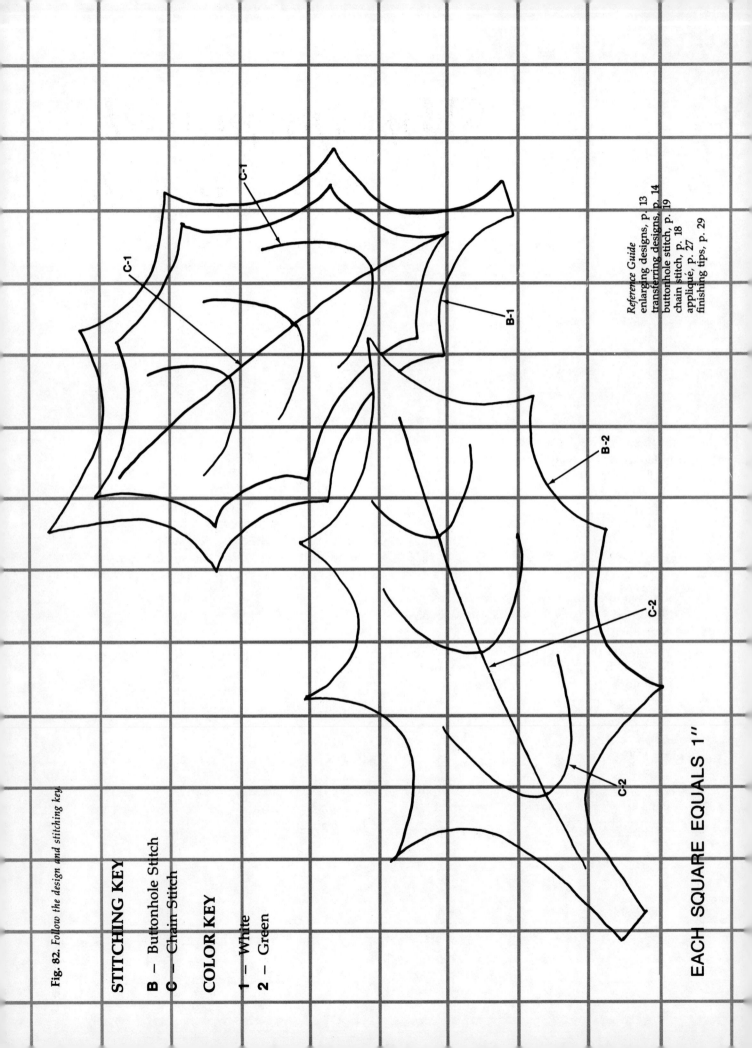

Fig. 82. *Follow the design and stitching key.*

STITCHING KEY

B – Buttonhole Stitch

C – Chain Stitch

COLOR KEY

1 – White

2 – Green

EACH SQUARE EQUALS 1"

Monogrammed towels

Shown in color on page 36.

Use your own initial to monogram your bath towels, hand towels and washcloths.

THE MATERIALS

Purple bath towels, hand towels and washcloths similar to the ones shown
3 skeins DMC #3 pearl cotton in the following colors and quantities: 1 skein green
#909, 1 skein yellow #744, 1 skein purple
#209
Small piece of organdy to embroider on

THE TOOLS

Equipment for enlarging and transferring the design, crewel or embroidery needle, small scissors, embroidery hoop

THE DESIGN

1. The design is shown in Figure 83. Use your own initial and incorporate the flower motif in the position most pleasing to your eye.

2. Transfer the floral design to the organdy and baste it in place on the towels.

THE EMBROIDERY

Put the work on the hoop and follow the stitching key.
1. Work all satin stitch areas first.
2. Next, work all stem stitch areas.
3. Do chain stitches last.

THE FINISHING

1. Lightly press with a steam iron on the wrong side.
2. Cut the organdy away carefully.

Fig. 83. *Follow the design and keys.*

PATTERN PIECES DRAWN SAME SIZE

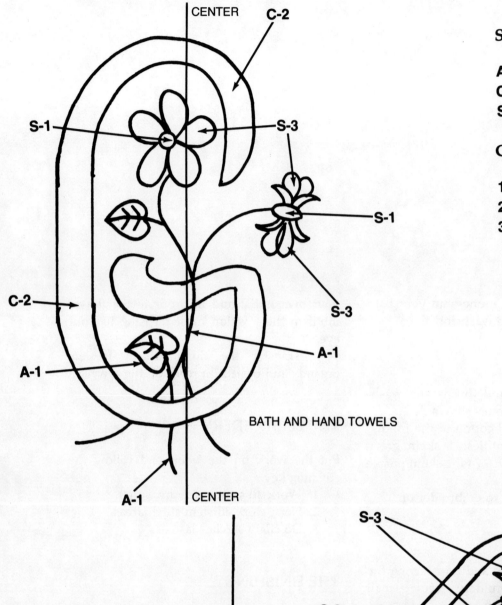

CENTER

C-2

S-1

S-3

C-2

A-1

S-1

S-3

A-1

BATH AND HAND TOWELS

A-1 CENTER

STITCHING KEY

A – Stem Stitch
C – Chain Stitch
S – Satin Stitch

COLOR KEY

1 – Green
2 – Yellow
3 – Purple

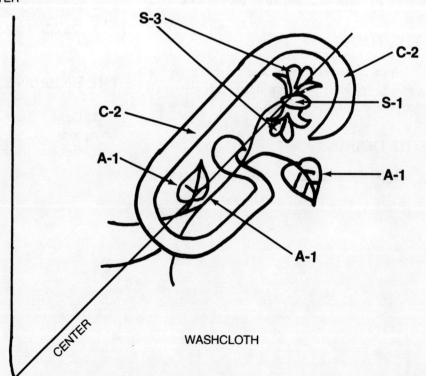

S-3

C-2

C-2

S-1

A-1

A-1

A-1

CENTER

WASHCLOTH